BEARA
A JOURNEY THROUGH HISTORY

Daniel M. O'Brien

Beara Historical Society

1991

Cover picture
'Summer Fields, Allihies' by Tim Goulding
© Tim Goulding 1986

First published in 1991 by
Beara Historical Society
Main Street,
Castletownbere,
Co. Cork.

© Beara Historical Society 1991
Reprinted March 1992

ISBN 0 9517862 0 2

Typesetting and printing by Litho Press Co., Midleton, Co. Cork.

CONTENTS

ACKNOWLEDGEMENTS

The Beara Historical Society gratefully acknowledges the assistance of the following in the publication of this book:

Cork Historical and Archaeological Society (for permission to reprint article)

Cork Archaeological Survey (photographs on pages 72, 73, 83, 104, 108 [ring fort], 111, 120, 131, 147 [site 132])

Connie Murphy, N.T. (photographs)

Gerard Harrington (photographs)

Tim Goulding (cover picture)

Penny Durell (editing)

Kieran Burke, Local History Librarian, Cork City Library (source identification)

Dr. Dáithi Ó hÓgáin, Dept. Irish Folklore, University College, Dublin. (source identification)

Cormac Boydell (geological information)

FOREWORD

Daniel Maddison O'Brien was a well-known and popular figure in Beara, appreciated and respected by all who knew him. He spent the latter part of his life as manager of the Castletownbere branch of the Munster and Leinster Bank and in retirement at Eyeries. Dan is remembered for a generosity of spirit and zest for life, and his enquiring mind was reflected in a wide range of interests, enthusiastically shared with others. He was a valuable asset to his adopted community: not the least of his achievements was conveying the importance of water safety and teaching many youngsters of the area to swim, a most practical benefit in a maritime environment. Dan enriched the cultural life of Beara through pioneering work in identifying archaeological sites and fostering historical interest, and in lectures and musical evenings.

As a tribute to his memory the Beara Historical Society is now pleased to publish Dan's writing on the history and archaeological sites of the barony of Beara. The Society was founded in November 1986. Our aims are to research and record the history of our area, to make known and preserve historical places and objects from the ravages of progress, to found a folk museum, and to provide a forum for literary endeavour in our community.

The beautiful Beara peninsula contains a precious legacy of the past that should be treasured: it is especially rich in archaeological remains, the memorials of bygone times, and has a wealth of historical associations.

Deep in the heart of each of us is a love of our own countryside, a landscape that portrays our history as far back as prehistoric times. It has taken more than 5,000 years to build up this valuable heritage of ancient monuments, which is now unfortunately becoming a dwindling inheritance, as seen in the lamentable destruction of ring forts, ancient cooking places, souterrains, megalithic tombs, burial mounds, standing stones, and stone circles.

As Dan O'Brien would have wished, we hope that *Beara: A Journey through History* will promote an increased awareness of the heritage in our landscape and encourage in its readers the desire to preserve all the historical material that still exists.

THE AUTHOR: AN APPRECIATION

When Daniel Maddison O'Brien joined what was then the Munster and Leinster Bank he was following a family tradition. Throughout my childhood I remember hearing the names of the places my father, my grandfather and my Uncle Dan had been stationed in. If other people had a sense of place, we had a sense of places, small towns and big towns of Ireland going back beyond our memory.

Kildysert, Roscrea, Limerick, Millstreet, Nenagh, Callan, Kilenaule, Mountrath, it was like a litany. But for my Uncle Dan, when he came to Castletownbere the litany stopped. He had found the place where he wanted to remain.

All of us remember summer holidays in the Beara peninsula with Uncle Dan. We spent the days spotting megaliths, seeing the copper mines at Allihies, walking the mountains. We came back in the evenings to listen to music in his cottage and browse through his collection of books. After spending time with my uncle, it became hard to ignore anything around you. Every stone had its significance, every flower its name, every road its story. He loved the Beara area for its wonderful natural beauty, its antiquity, and of course, its people. I like to think his book was a tribute to a place which had made him happy.

To me his most memorable quality was his enthusiasm for knowledge and his joy in sharing that knowledge. It is good to know that the information he collected over so many years is available now and may give the same pleasure to others that it gave to him.

Harriet O'Carroll
May 1991

Daniel M. O'Brien (1911-1989)

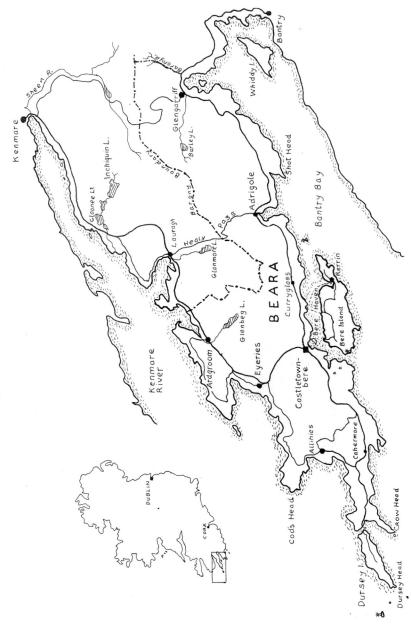

SKETCH-MAP OF BEARA PENINSULA

Bantry

Whiddy I.

Glengarriff

Barley L.

Shot Head

Bantry Bay

Adrigole

Kenmare

Sheen R.

Barony R.

Boundary

Barony

Inchiquin L.

Cloonee Lᵗˢ

Pass

Healy

Laragh

Glanmore L.

Retrin

Curryglass

BEARA

Ardgroom

Glenbeg L.

Bere Haven

Bere Island

Eyeries

Castletown-
bere

Kenmare
River

Allihies

Cahermore

Cods Head

Crow Head

Dursey I.

Dursey Head

DUBLIN

CORK

8

Introduction

The Barony of Beara

The term 'Barony' was introduced by the Normans when, on their invasion of England, they adopted the Saxon land measurement of Thane. It also appears to have been more or less synonymous with the Welsh Cantref and the Celtic Tricha cet and would seem to have applied to military tenure, supplying thirty hundreds of soldiers. This also resembles Roman custom and the denominations of hundreds and thirty hundreds used by the Greeks, Germans and Celts in the period 600 B.C. to 200 B.C. and may be traced to Indo-European military traditions.[1]

Charles Smith, writing in 1750, states: 'Bear and Bantry compose but one barony'.[2] However, in 1700 the Protestant bishop of the united diocese of Cork and Ross, Dive Downes, in 'Visitation of His Diocese' refers to the half barony of Bear, and it is also mentioned in several deeds of the 18th century as being a half barony. This was probably due to the understandable difficulty of obtaining a force of 3,000 fighting men from the barren mountains of Beara. Nor in the time of the Norman invasion could such a force have been considered reliable. Possibly the military aspect of the barony was allowed to run down and the administration of the feudal knights' fees more effectively organized from the newly founded counties and shires.

Certainly the baronies continued to be used as a territorial division for the great surveys connected with the Cromwellian confiscations, the Civil Survey and the Down Survey of Sir William Petty, and it was at this period that the baronies were further divided into parishes and townlands. They were used in the 18th and 19th centuries for the introduction of county rule by the Grand Jury system, and the Grand Jury Act of 1836 authorized the holding of sessions in each barony; they were also used for the collection of the county rate levied to build roads. The barony was used as a census division up to 1901, but with the reorganization of local government of the post-Famine period it gradually dropped out of use.

The barony of Beara covers 89,986 statute acres. Its population was as follows:

1851	19,909
1861	16,503
1871	15,807
1881	15,242
1891	13,961
1901	12,602

But to get back to basic beginnings!

Most of the rocks of the Beara peninsula belong to the Upper Old Red Sandstone series, which are around 365 million years old. South Munster was very different in those days - a flat and featureless semi-desert with seasonal lakes and south-flowing rivers. Far to the north a Himalayan-size mountain chain stretched from Norway to Northern Ireland and across to North America. As the elements wore these great mountains away sands, silts and dust were carried southward in seasonal flood rivers. Over many millions of years these sediments accumulated on flood plains and in large seasonal lakes, and consolidated to form the sandstones, siltstones and slates of Beara.

About 50 to 60 million years after this time horizontal compressional forces in the Earth's crust caused the familiar folding and faulting of the Beara bedrock. This is best seen along the coast of the north of Allihies.

There is no further mark of the geological history until the predominantly arctic deposits, between 2 million and 10,000 years ago. During part of this time an independent ice pack covered almost the whole of Cork and west Kerry. At the onset of a more temperate climate this ice sheet began to melt and the ice on the northern side of the Kerry mountains moved down into the Kerry lowlands, while that on the southern side of these mountains and in the Kenmare River moved over the Caha and Slieve Miskish mountains into Bantry Bay, which was filled with ice. This ice escaped northeastward into the mountain valleys, and southwestward into the open sea. Some of these valleys, such as those of Coomhola, Snave and Cousane, were filled with ice already, which probably came in from the north. Further pressure was put on the ice in Bantry Bay by the glacial overflow valley from Drimoleague to Bantry, where the present main road between these two places runs and where the railway formerly ran.

When the Bantry Bay ice sheet passed over the Pass of Keimaneigh it formed a terminal moraine from there to Skibbereen and then it broke away from the parent ice mass on the Caha mountains. When ice breaks away from its parent mass it dies, without any forward movement to form a moraine. When this vast weight of ice melted from off the mountain tops the land level rose, which accounts for so many rivers of Beara flowing over a waterfall into the sea.

There are many signs of glacial activity in Beara. Striae (lines on the rocks showing the direction in which the ice moved) may be found everywhere. West of Glengarriff there are a large number of glacial erratics (rocks deposited on the mountain side by the moving ice). Other signs of ice activity are the glacial valleys of Cloonee, Glenbeg and

Glenmore with their impressive lakes, and the valley of Kilmacowen, where in several quarries there may be observed alternate bands of fine clay and gravel, indicating periods of fast and slow movement of the ice.[3]

The Beara peninsula is particularly rich in prehistoric archaeological remains, and the process of identifying and recording these sites is by no means completed. I have examined and listed some 180 sites, often assisted by young people of the area, and 151 of the sites are included in my article ' A List of Some Archaeological Sites on the Berehaven Peninsula', *JCHAS* vol. 75 No. 221 (1970), pp. 12-24. This article provides map co-ordinates, and by kind permission of the Cork Historical and Archaeological Society it is reproduced in Appendix A of this book. I apply the same numbering system to the sites mentioned in the book.

A useful source for the study of Beara archaeology is by Denis O'Shea and Gerard Crowley, 'The Archaeology of Berehaven', Project No. 53, Full Life for Youth Scheme, Kerry Diocese, 1972. There are manuscript copies there and in Cork County Library, Bantry, Archaeological Department, University College Cork, and the Cork Historical and Archaeological Society.

While many of the sites I describe are accessible, I suggest that it would be appropriate to ask permission of the owners before venturing onto their lands.

Editor's note. Several place names have spelling variations - the official version and the form in common use. Examples are Ballynacarriga/Ballinacarriga, Caherkeen/Caherkeem, Cloan/Cluin, Drom/Droum, Garinish/Garnish, Fanahy/Finaha, Loughanemore/ Lehanmore, Reentrusk/Reentrisk, and Urhin/Urhan.

SKETCH-MAP OF GLENGARRIFF AREA

TOWNLANDS

1. Rougham
2. Derreenavroonig
3. Currakillane
4. Youngfield
5. Doorus
6. Lyre
7. Rossnagrena
8. Tooreen
9. Crossterry East
10. Canrooska
11. Derreennagough
12. Coonane
13. Crossterry West
14. Lickeen West
15. Lickeen East
16. Derreenboy Upper
17. Derreenboy Lower
18. Dromdour
19. Skehil
20. Derreenagarig
21. Carrigrour
22. Currakeal
23. Gortroe Upper
24. Gortroe Lower
25. Glengarriff
26. Esknamucky
27. Drumaclarig
28. Cappyaughna
29. Monteensudder
30. Reenmeen West
31. Reenmeen East
32. Rossnashunsoge
33. Dromderaown
34. Coomarkane
35. Derrynafulla
36. Coorannel
37. Shrone
38. Derryconnery
39. Inchintaggart
40. Furkeal
41. Muccurragh
42. Bocarnagh

Chapter 1

Bantry Bay

The boundary between the barony of Bantry and that of Beara is the little Barony River that flows down from the Coomhola Mountain to fall into the sea just east of Glengarriff. It was, incidentally, at this point that I saw the only pine marten I have ever seen. What a pity it would be if this beautiful animal should become extinct.

Glengarriff has for many years now been a popular and well-known holiday resort and needs little publicity. When he visited the place in 1842 the writer William Makepeace Thackeray, undaunted by torrents of rain and his portmanteau being sent back to Cork in error, speaks of the 'astonishing beauty of the country' and wonders 'what sends picturesque tourists to the Rhine and Saxon Switzerland? Within five miles round the pretty inn of Glengarriff there is a country of the magnificence of which no pen can give an idea'.[1] Later he mentions 'Mr. Eccles', the proprietor of the inn. The Registry of Deeds (Dublin) states that on 25 March 1836 Thomas Eccles leased from the Earl of Bantry '23 acres 2 roods lands of Reenmeen or Reenmeen east, on which plot the Glengarriff Inn or Eccles Hotel is built, for 200 years at a rent of £12.8.3 per annum.'

When Thackeray visited there in 1842 a two-horse car for travellers ran three times a week from Bantry to Killarney by way of Glengarriff and Kenmare. He paints a very vivid picture of how thickly populated the country appeared to be.

To the left of the road to Castletownbere, as one crosses the bridge leading from Glengarriff, beyond the old bridge will be seen an ancient ruined bridge. This is known as Cromwell's Bridge and of it the travellers Mr. and Mrs. S. C. Hall heard the following tale in 1840:

> When Oliver Cromwell was passing through the Glen to visit the
> O'Sullivans he had so much trouble in getting across the narrow
> but rushing river that he told the inhabitants if they did not
> build him a bridge by the time he returned, he would hang up a
> man for every hours delay he met with. 'So the bridge was
> ready agin he came back', quoth our informant, 'for they knew
> the ould villain to be a man of his word'.[2]

The bridge probably predates Cromwell and, according to Rev. Horatio Townsend, it would appear that it was still in use when he wrote in 1810: 'It (the river) is passed by a good stone bridge, attributed to Cromwell, and still bearing his name, though it should seem that nothing be gained on the west side of the river could have been worth the trouble of the undertaking'.[3]

The old name for the place where the bridge is erected was *Ceim an Ghabhair*, meaning 'goat's pass', probably where goats jumped across the river before the bridge was built.

Westward the road climbs steadily up from Glengarriff, crossing Magannagan Bridge and leaving the typically glacial Loughavaul lakes to the south, until at Coolieragh Hill (121m) the highest point of the road between Glengarriff and Castletownbere is reached. Here a steep escarpment runs up west of the Glen of Glengarriff to meet the Kerry boundary at the tunnels on the Glengarriff-Kenmare road; through this point also runs a barometric pressure line, west of which the rainfall averages 1000-1500 mm and east of it 1500-2000 mm. This would appear to be a natural boundary but the paucity of good land west of Glengarriff made its inclusion in the barony an economic necessity.

From here a very extensive view of Bantry Bay will be seen, eastward to Bantry across Whiddy Island, scene of the *Betelgeuse* disaster of the night of 8 January 1979, and westward, along the craggy backbone of the Caha and Slieve Miskish mountains to the open sea. Nearly 400 years ago another disaster that took two years to complete ended in Bantry Bay.

One Thomas Cavendish made a successful voyage around the world in the years 1586 to 1588 from which he returned a wealthy man. He was not long in dissipating his fortune and by 1591 it became necessary for him to replenish his coffers and this he proposed doing by a voyage in search of a southwest passage, which would also give him ample opportunity for raiding the treasure ships of the Spanish Main. However, this time his luck was out, for not only did he lose his life on the venture but it became known as 'the world's worst voyage'.

In his ship the *Leicester* and accompanied by the famous navigator Captain John Davis in the *Desire* (the ship in which he had made his voyage in 1586 to 1588), and three other boats, the *Roebuck*, the *Dainty* and the *Black*, he set sail from Plymouth on 6 August 1591. Fate went against the expedition and it would seem that Cavendish was not a man who could stand up to adversity. He quarrelled with his master and others on the *Leicester* and transferred his flag to the *Desire*. This was bound to be unsatisfactory and, sure enough, Cavendish would not accept the advice of Davis, who, even then, was held to be the best navigator in the world and who in later years made great contributions to the science of navigation. Cavendish returned to his own vessel and, apparently in a huff, sailed out of sight.

On two occasions 25 of Cavendish's crew were slain when they landed to seek food, and, to make matters worse, the cowardly master of the *Roebuck*, with provisions for six months for 120 persons although there were only 46 on board, stole away leaving 10 of his crew ashore, and got back to Ireland before any of the other vessels.

Cavendish landed on the island of Ascension, from where he wrote to Sir Tristram Gorges, sole executor of his will, claiming that Davis had run away from him and was the cause of the failure of the expedition. He died there in 1592.

Having failed to overtake the *Leicester* and not finding that vessel in either Port Desire or the Straits of Magellan, Davis began to prepare for the voyage home. In June 1592 a petition to the Almighty was drawn up, praying for their safe return home. It was signed by 40 members of the crew then surviving.

Attempts were then made to provision the ship with eggs, penguins, young seals, young gulls and other birds. They also got scurvy-grass which they fried with eggs, using train oil instead of butter. This they found very good for curing swellings and for their general improvement in health.

On 22 December 1592 they put out from Port Desire, having anchored off the Penguin Isle where they took aboard 14,000 of the dried birds. On 30 January 1593 they called to the Isle of Placencia for provisions but the inhabitants had fled taking with them all meal and livestock.

In this raid more of Davis's men were killed and when he eventually set sail across the Atlantic only 27 of his crew remained to work the ship. Food, in spite of the most stringent rationing, ran out, and when they resorted to the dried penguins it was found that these had been imperfectly cured and had gone bad. As one of the survivors graphically describes the position:

> There bred in them a most lothsome and ugly worme of an inch long. This worme did so mightily increase and devoure our victuals that there was in reason no hope how we should avoide famine, but be devoured of these wicked creatures; there was nothing that they did not devoure, only yron excepted; our clothes, boots, shooes, hats, shirts, stockings; and for the ship, they did so eat the timbers, as that we greatly feared they would undoe us by gnawing through the ship's side. Great was the care and diligence of our captaine, master, and company, to consume these vermin; but the more we laboured to kill them the more they increased; so that at last we could not sleep for them, but they would eate our flesh and bite like mosquitoes.[4]

When they crossed the equator they were stricken by a fresh crop of diseases and some went mad and jumped overboard. A fresh fall of rain saved the lives of more, yet when on 11 June 1593 the storm-tossed ship put into Berehaven only 16 (of whom only five could work the ship) remained of the 76 persons on board when the ship left Plymouth two years before. The wretched crew were carried ashore by the locals (for which they were charged £10) and Captain Davis and his master found their way back to Padstow in Cornwall on board a fishing boat. One wonders what happened to the rest of the crew.

Poor Davis's troubles were not at an end, however, for when he got to his home at Sandridge he found that his wife had deserted their three young sons (Davis's will, dated 12 October 1604, mentions his sons Gilbert, Arthur and Philip) and had run off with another man. Davis remained at home for two years during which he wrote his famous books *The Seaman's Secrets* and *The World's Hypographical Description;* he improved the cross-staff and invented the back-staff and was probably the first of the world's scientific navigators. It was extraordinary that the reputation of such a brilliant seaman could have been so blighted by the ravings of Cavendish's crazed mind. In 1595 he sailed as chief pilot of the first expedition of the Dutch East India Company and then joined the British East India Company. He was killed by pirates off the coast of Malacca or Borneo in 1605.

In April 1689 a naval personage of a very different character to that of Captain John Davis arrived in Bantry Bay. Admiral Herbert had been cruising with his fleet along the south coasts of England and Ireland waiting for a French convoy, which his scouts sighted on 29 April. According to one account, Herbert was advised that the French fleet had put into Baltimore and he arrived there only to find that the ships had put to sea again, so he followed them into Bantry Bay where he had an indecisive engagement with them.

Another account says he was advised that they had gone into Baltimore, so he put into Bantry and, to his dismay, found the French ships there. This latter account would seem to be more in keeping with Herbert's character for, as a popular jingle of the day had it, he was noted for being where the enemy were not. Anyway, the engagement was received as a victory by both the English and the French but, it would appear, Herbert did not seem inclined to discuss the affair and soon after we find the famous diarist, Samuel Pepys, father of the British navy, being requested to make a report to the committees of both Houses of Parliament as to the action in Bantry Bay on 1 May 1689, showing Admiral Herbert's strength in ships, men and guns, and his losses in killed and wounded, ship by ship. This resulted in another query, as to why Admiral Herbert had only 20 ships in the engagement.

Bantry Bay seems to have been an unfortunate place for invasions but most of the failures, when they were not due to the behaviour of a man like Herbert, seem to have been caused by bad weather, internal disputes and the resultant delay in departure until an unpropitious time.

The Spanish fleet for the invasion of Kinsale was ready to set sail in June 1601, but there was some disagreement about the composition of the army and navy personnel. Then further delay was caused by a report that an English squadron had sailed south to intercept a large and valuable Spanish convoy, with gold and treasure from the American Indies, which was then due at the Azores, and some of the invasion fleet were diverted to protect this convoy and see it safely into port; so eventually it was the middle of September before the fleet got under way. On 23 September the Council of Ireland, under the new Lord Deputy, Charles Blount, Lord Mountjoy, was seated in Kilkenny when it received a report that the Spanish under Don Juan del Aguila had landed at Kinsale and taken the town without opposition. But this force, which when it left the river Tagus consisted of 6,000 men in 15 armed vessels and 30 transports, had suffered severely at sea and by the time it reached Kinsale was reduced to 3,400 men. Then started the usual recriminations!

Del Aguila was a brave but testy, passionate and suspicious officer and he was bitterly disappointed that only O'Sullivan Beare, O'Driscoll and O'Connor of Kerry declared openly for the Spanish forces, while they heard daily of chiefs who they had expected to be their allies but were now either prisoners or allies of the English. On the other side the Spaniards were criticized for landing so far south and so dangerously near the English arsenal and headquarters at Cork, while their northern allies, including O'Neill, O'Donnell and Doherty, were kept busy on their own frontiers and could not give the immediate assistance that was so vitally necessary.

On 17 October, three weeks after they had landed, the Spanish found themselves besieged by a mixed army of English and Anglo-Irish, 15,000 strong. This siege lasted 10 weeks and on 12 January, nineteen days after the battle of Kinsale, Don Juan del Aguila surrendered the town and agreed to hand over the castles of Dunboy, Baltimore and Castlehaven. As regards Dunboy, Donal Cam O'Sullivan Beare and his followers tunnelled their way into the castle while the Spaniards slept and deprived them of it. This so annoyed del Aguila that he offered to attack Dunboy and hand it over to the English, but the Lord President of Munster, Sir George Carew, said the sooner he saw the back of Don Juan's heels the better! After this followed the siege of Dunboy. (See Chapters 7 and 10).

Possibly the most disastrous of the invasions of Bantry Bay was that of the French under General Hoche at the end of December 1796. On 1 February 1796 Theobald Wolfe Tone, an Irish barrister and a leader of the revolutionary United Irishmen movement, arrived at Le Havre from New York with the intention of persuading the French to invade Ireland.

The French Directory proved favourably inclined to the idea but would send no more than 5,000 men, while Tone pleaded for 20,000. Then, in July, Tone met the young General Hoche who was very enthusiastic and assured Tone he would go in sufficient force. Napoleon was always suspicious of the Irish and no doubt it was he who persuaded the Directory to send an agent to Ireland to satisfy themselves that all was as represented by Tone.

At length, early in December the fleet was ready and put to sea on the 16th: 17 sail of line, 13 frigates, and 13 smaller ships, carrying 15,000 picked troops well supplied with artillery and munitions of war. Tone was in the *Indomptable*, 80 guns, commanded by a Canadian named Bédout; the commander of the forces, General Hoche, and the admiral were on board the *Fraternité*. Again, it was too late in the year for such an expedition and on the third morning, after groping about and losing each other in fog, half the fleet found themselves off the Kerry coast and put into Bantry Bay where they anchored for three or four days. Unfortunately, the *Fraternité* was amongst the missing ships and Bouvet, the vice-admiral, was opposed to moving without his chief, while the second in command, Grouchy, was irresolute and nervous. Eventually, on Christmas Day, it was decided to disembark on the following morning; but, once again, the British-biased Bantry weather took a hand and during the night it blew a half gale that had increased to almost hurricane force by morning and the vice-admiral ordered the fleet to slip anchor and stand out to sea. Soon the ships were all driven off the Irish coast and the major portion of the fleet, with Grouchy and Tone, arrived in Brest on New Year's Day. General Hoche and the admiral only arrived in La Rochelle on 15 January 1797. Rarely was an opportunity so badly missed!

Samuel Bayley, the customs officer of Berehaven, in a letter dated 22 December 1796 to Richard White says: 'The French Fleet are at this moment beating up the harbour for Bantry, 28 ships of line and a number of smaller vessels; what are we to do! What will become of us God only knows!!'

One man who did try to save the situation was Captain Daniel O'Sullivan of Coulagh on the Kenmare River, an ex-officer in the British army and of whom it is said that he was the last titular O'Sullivan Beare, though this statement must be accepted with reserve. Captain Daniel mustered 200 peasants (another source says 2,000 but this seems unlikely) and drove all the cattle and removed all provisions inland out of reach of the French, as well as informing Richard White of Bantry and his own uncle, Maurice O'Connell of Derrynane, Co. Kerry, of the invasion and capturing a lieutenant and boat crew. Daniel O'Sullivan Beare took these captives to Bantry where General Dalrymple had arrived with a very small force, only half a regiment. The general had refused to believe that the ships in the bay were really French until O'Sullivan produced his prisoners, whereupon Dalrymple immediately retreated to Cork.

Captain Daniel O'Sullivan Beare died on a sea journey from Bristol to Cork and his obituary appeared in the *Gentleman's Magazine* 1814 p. 43. It tells of his exploits at the time of the French invasion, for which he was made a Freeman of Cork, the first Roman Catholic to be so honoured since the reign of Queen Anne. His own boat, valued at £300, was sunk by the French, and he was presented with a handsome sword by the citizens of Cork.

While the dispersal of the fleet through gales, fogs and plain misunderstandings meant a reduction in its strength from 14,000 men to 6,382, if Grouchy had plucked enough courage to land before Christmas he would have met with no opposition, since there was not a military man within 40 miles of Bantry Bay. If the French had succeeded in landing the best the English could have mustered were 2,000 men in Bandon and, according to the parliamentary debates, there were not 3,000 men available to meet the French. Sir John Moore (of Corunna fame) in 1797 gave the military forces in Ireland as:

Regulars and Fencibles	18,601
Militia	21,590
English & Irish artillery	1,600
Yeomanry	35,000
Total	76,791[5]

Beresford, a leading official in the government, said: 'We had two days after the French were at anchor in Bantry Bay, from Cork to Bantry, less than 3,000 men, two pieces of artillery and no magazine of any kind, no hospital, no provisions; it was clear that Cork was gone.'[6]

Generally, the blame for the disaster had been placed on the bad navigation and seamanship of the French navy and lack of co-operation with the army. But it would seem that some of the blame must fall on Tone himself. It is an understandable tendency for one in his position to paint a rosy picture of the prospects of success and, in his first report to the French Directory, Tone claimed that not less than 200,000 men had been raised in Ireland for the British forces, of which 80,000 were for the navy alone, and he expected that these would desert on the landing of the French. Actually, the total number of officers, sailors and marines at the beginning of 1796 was only just over 20,000, of which between 16,000 and 17,000 had been recruited in Ireland. This misrepresentation of the size of an army he might expect to meet could have had, on such a nervous and indecisive person as Grouchy, the reverse effect to that hoped for.

The French traveller de Latocnaye, who travelled to Bantry in 1797, said he had stayed at Dunmanway with Mr. Cox and that there were 'in this little town two hundred French republican officers, prisoners on parole, and I was glad to have the opportunity to know what kind of people these men might be. At Mr. Cox's house I dined with two or three of them, and found them polite enough.'[7]

The Dutch, or as it was then known, the Batavian Republic had a powerful fleet and an unemployed army and was willing to listen to any proposals that might restore Holland to its former glory. The agent of the Irish Directory approached the Batavian government and suggested an invasion of Ireland. Tone had a high opinion of this agent, Edward John Lewines, a Dublin lawyer, and accompanied him to The Hague, where the proposal was discussed and agreed to.

There were in the Texel 16 ships of line and 10 frigates, victualled for three months, with 15,000 men and 80 field guns on board, ready to sail after the usual disagreements had been ironed out, and on 8 July 1797 Tone was on board the flagship, the *Vryheid*; but the winds proved even more adverse than ever and when, by the end of August, a favourable wind had not sprung up and all the victuals had been eaten, the Dutch Directory decided to land the troops and postpone the expedition.

The French were not all dismayed by the Bantry Bay failure and, in fact, were rather encouraged by having cruised around the Irish coast for so long without encountering the British navy. They assured the Irish contingent that the invasion was not abandoned but merely postponed. The hopes of the Irish were again raised when, in October 1797, a decree was passed by the French Directory for the formation of 'the Army of England,' with Napoleon Buonaparte as commander-in-chief and Desaix as his second in command. Every assurance was given that the expedition against England would never be abandoned, and all winter busy preparations went ahead in the ports of Le Havre, La Rochelle and Brest and also, rather ominously and somewhat mystifying to the Irish, at the Mediterranean port of Toulon. Then, on 20 May 1798, within three days of the outbreak of revolution in Dublin, Wexford and Kildare, the expedition set sail, but not for Ireland. The 'Army of England' had suddenly become the 'Army of Egypt', an error of judgment that Napoleon was to bitterly regret and he is recorded as having said, during his imprisonment at St. Helena, 'If instead of the expedition to Egypt, I had undertaken that to Ireland, what could England do now? On such chances,' he mournfully added, 'depend the destinies of empires.'[8]

There are in the various accounts of this Bantry Bay invasion several discrepancies which I very much regret not having been able to do any research work on. In a couple of accounts (e.g. *An Invasion that Failed: the French Expedition to Ireland* by Commander E.H. Stuart Jones, Oxford, 1950) a list is given of some 35 English ships of war that were said to have been in Bantry Bay when the French were at anchor there in 1796, and, in an obituary notice of John Westropp Carey, who died at Glenlough near Bantry on 3 June 1862, the *Cork Constitution* says of him that he was the last survivor of seven brothers who served their country in either naval or military capacity. 'Lionel Carey, the fourth brother, was lieutenant on board H.M.S. "Pearl", chased the French from Bantry, and died from fever in the East Indies while in the service.' But in the lists of British naval vessels said to be in Bantry Bay on this occasion no 'Pearl' appears.

But to return to the hill of Coolieragh and resume meanderings from there.

SKETCH-MAP OF ADRIGOLE AREA

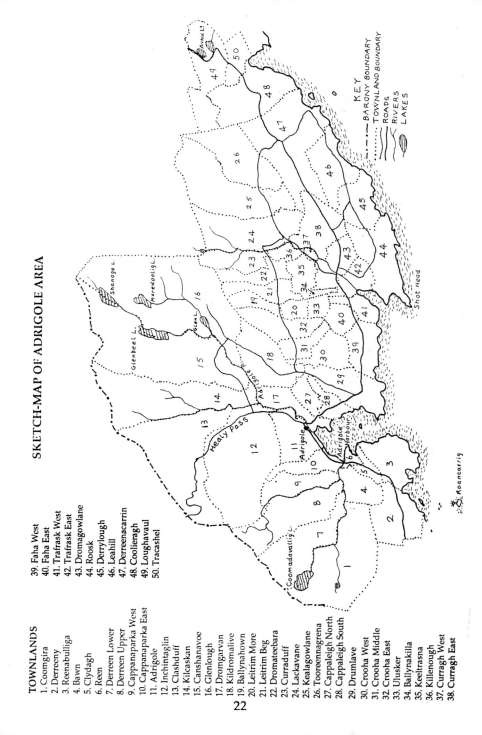

TOWNLANDS

1. Coomgira
2. Derreeny
3. Reenabulliga
4. Bawn
5. Clydagh
6. Reen
7. Derreen Lower
8. Derreen Upper
9. Cappanaparka West
10. Cappanaparka East
11. Adrigole
12. Inchintaglin
13. Clashduff
14. Kilcaskan
15. Canshanavoe
16. Glenlough
17. Dromgarvan
18. Kildromalive
19. Ballynahown
20. Leitrim More
21. Leitrim Beg
22. Dromateebara
23. Curraduff
24. Lackavane
25. Kealagowlane
26. Tooreennagrena
27. Cappaleigh North
28. Cappaleigh South
29. Drumlave
30. Crooha West
31. Crooha Middle
32. Crooha East
33. Ulusker
34. Ballynakilla
35. Keeltrasna
36. Killenough
37. Curragh West
38. Curragh East
39. Faha West
40. Faha East
41. Trafrask West
42. Trafrask East
43. Dromagowlane
44. Roosk
45. Derrylough
46. Leahill
47. Derreenacarrin
48. Coolieragh
49. Loughavaul
50. Tracashel

Chapter 2

Cromwellian Period

From Coolieragh the road slopes slowly down to the sea past the former national school of Derrincorrin. About 200m beyond the school a road branches to the right, up into the mountains, and just around the next corner, still on the main road, another road branches seawards to the left down to Zetland pier. This is a pleasant place for a picnic or boating, and about three fields to the southwest will be found a small but sheltered sandy beach. The road continues past the pier, to climb over the ridge of the hill to rejoin the main road at Trafrask, a detour well worth doing from the scenic point of view. The hill between the roads is Derrincorrin, or the 'oakwood of the cairn,' and the cairn (or pile of stones) on top of it may very well be a prehistoric burial place.

Returning again to Derrincorrin School, the more adventurous driver may like to take the aforementioned first road to the right. It goes in about 300-400m and then turns sharply west running along the base of the mountain. After about another 500m a by-road branches to the right and steeply zigzags up until it joins another, older road at right angles, about 100m higher up the mountain side. The older road branches east and west and was the old road from Castletownbere to Glengarriff and Cork. The road to the west is still in use but the portion to the east is now a mere track; however, it makes a very attractive route for walking to Glengarriff, where it comes down at the head of the glen.

The road that zigzags up to join this old road is known (and is so marked on the Ordnance Survey six inch map) as 'Cromwell's Road', traditionally said to have been built by Cromwell's troops. The latter statement has been disputed by some people on the plea that Cromwell's troops were never in Beara but this can easily be disproved, for it is on record that Reendisert Court, an O'Sullivan Beare house, was destroyed 'by a ship of war in Cromwell's time' and there are several references to Beara and Daniel O'Sullivan Beare in the Cromwell correspondence. In a letter from the Commissioner to the Speaker, dated March 1653, it is reported that a small force of Cromwellians was intercepted by O'Sullivan Beare and Colonel O'Driscoll and the captain and 34 men were killed.

That very thorough researcher, the late Mr. John T. Collins, has said: 'So far as West Cork is concerned there is no record of any transplantation. There was a certain infiltration of Cromwellian grantees, some of whom were glad to retain the former owners as tenants.'[1] The principal of these infiltrators would appear to have been Major George Walters, Peter Wallis and Joseph Deane, who are mentioned in a court case (circa 1783-86), a copy of which is among the Hutchins family papers and also among the P. O'Keefe MSS in Cork County Library, Cork. A letter from Cromwell dated 14 November 1654 authorizes in compensation of Major Peter Wallis, for his losses in transporting the Irish into Spain.[2]

Shortly before this, on 12 May 1654, Cromwell orders that 'the line of protection in Co. Cork be not enlarged inasmuch as it appears there is waste land enough within the said line for the use of the said inhabitants.'[3]   More definite still is a letter from Cromwell dated 16 March 1653, saying 'the enemy in Kerry do still increase... having lately taken an island called the Dorzes. A strong party sent down by land to reduce them and Captain Sherwin ordered to go thither by sea.[4]

Local tradition says the Cromwellian troops landed at Mehal Head, Roosk, about two km south of Cromwell's Road. In correspondence about a grant to Sir Robert Collingwood, in the months of January to March 1659, the Lord Protector, Richard Cromwell (who succeeded his father in 1658 but resigned the post within eight months and died in 1712, aged 88) consents to alter his resolution and instead of property in the town of Drogheda orders that land to that amount at soldiers' rates be set out in the baronies of Beara and Bantry. However, this letter 'not being in due form the Irish Council desired it should come under the proper seal and with "such testes" are as usual.'[5]   The name Collingwood does not appear in Beara and it is probable that the corrected letter was not received back at all.

For somewhat more modern references to the Cromwellian army in Beara: in the 'Visitation of His Diocese' in the year 1700 Bishop Dive Downes says, 'At Dunbwy als Beerehaven, there was a castle in Qn Elizabeth's time, it was made a fort in Cromwell's time.'[6] Samuel Lewis, in his *Topographical Dictionary of Ireland*, published 1837, states (vol. 1 p. 308), 'Many silver coins have been found at Ross McOwen including one of Cromwell's, and in vol. 2 p. 166 he says, 'on the same river, near its influx to the bay, are the ruined gables of the castle of Rindisart, the stronghold of Sir Owen O'Sullivan which was taken by Ireton in the parliamentary war, and by his order demolished.'

The final and most recent proof of the presence of Cromwellian troops in Beara was found in the summers of 1967 and 1973, when Dunboy fort was excavated by the late Dr. E. M. Fahy, then of the Geographical Department of University College, Cork. The excavations revealed the remains of a seventeenth-century star-shaped fort. The foregoing should be sufficient to discountenance the theory that, in this case, 'Cromwell' was a corruption of two Irish words meaning 'sharp bends'!

It may be queried why Cromwell's Road was built at all. Well, the road which we travelled from Derrincorrin and which ran along the base of the mountain over rock outcrop continues on to contact the present Glengarriff-Castletownbere road at Trafrask but, after passing where Cromwell's Road commences, at Killenough, the land becomes marshy with many small streams and would have been unsuitable for moving heavy guns. It would have been even more unsuitable for siege equipment. Since Cromwell's campaign in Ireland was based on speed, siege equipment, especially when, as was the case here, it was drawn by oxen, would have slowed him down too much.

The main piece of siege equipment used by the Irish was the 'sow', a kind of house built on wheels, with a very thickly padded roof. It was pushed up against the defensive walls and the roof protected those underneath while they tunnelled away at the base of the castle wall. It is known that while Cromwell did on occasion use the sow, it certainly was not in regular use by his army. In fact he rarely used the heavier field guns such as the culverin or demi-culverin and both in England and Ireland the bulk of the guns used by the Cromwellian armies were light field pieces called sakers, minions and drakes. The first fired a ball weighing five or six pounds, the second one of three and a half pounds and the drake probably a three pounder, or even smaller. All these could be fired about 15 times an hour.

The road running east and west up to which Cromwell's Road climbs is very old; it is certainly medieval and, as there are a large number of antiquities bordering it, it may even have been a prehistoric route way. A line of standing stones, both large and small and standing at various distances apart, may be traced almost the whole length of the peninsula parallel to such of this road as is still in use and to the remants of it that may still be traced in fields and commons lands. Where the zigzags of Cromwell's Road reach the old medieval road the latter rapidly becomes a lane leading east down between Sugarloaf Mountain (575m) and Gowlbeg Mountain (359m) into the great glen and forest of Glengarriff: a most spectacular and yet comparatively easy walk or ride, any rivers having bridges over them. A wonderful contribution towards increasing tourism would be to bring these old medieval roads back into use as tracks for walking, mountain climbing and horse trekking. The old roads run about 100m higher up the mountains than the present roads and can be traced all around the peninsula, from Glengarriff on the south, along the southern sides of the Caha and Slieve Miskish mountains to the furthest point of the peninsula at Dursey, and back around the northern side to Lauragh and Glenmore.

Chapter 3

Adrigole

Here at the junction of the Cromwellian and the medieval roads, if we look back east we can see a large standing stone on the skyline and another, about 30m further down, between which the old road ran. To the west the road crosses over a wild and rocky stream. In the next field west of this stream and to the north of the road will be found a much weathered rath, or earthen ring fort. The main point of interest is that it can be seen where a small stream was diverted to fill the fosse, or trench around the rath. A few hundred metres further on, to the south side of the road, there is another fine standing stone to be seen. A little to the west we come to a junction south (Leitrim Cross): opposite there is a gate, on the north side of the road; go in here and walk about 500m up the hillside to find a very nice small wedge grave, marked on the Ordnance Survey map as a 'cromlech'. There is a splendid view from here. On the opposite side of the road in the second field, close to some farm buildings and hiding behind a wall, is a small standing stone.

Another 500m or so along our western road will bring us to a bridge over a small stream, alongside which a lane runs down to a field, and in the next field to this, on the other side of the stream, is an interesting group of standing stones, probably a collapsed megalithic tomb of some kind. Nearby is a standing stone, whose top edge slopes to the west, and if one looks up the slope a fine fort will be seen a couple of fields away. Unfortunately, the last time I visited this site, the gap into the field had been blocked and it was not possible to get through, but it may be accessible from the small standing stone above or from the next site to the west.

A little further to the west we come to a group of houses at Crooha East, beside a road running southwards. A couple of hundred metres down this road on the left (eastern) side there is a very impressive ring fort. Little is left of the interior, though the entrance to the filled-in souterrain may be traced, and circular patches of different-coloured grass indicate where huts have been, and some hut sites may also be traced on the interior of the earthen embankment. On the southeastern side the fosse is very deep and, with the high and steep defensive embankment, it is most impressive. In the adjoining field to the northeast is a circular mound, with no embankment and only faint traces of a fosse. Archaeologists were slow to accept this as an antiquity, though three engineers confirmed that the mound was artificial, and eventually the local name (Lisbeg, or the little fort) proved to the

Inscribed circle-enclosed cross, Crooha West (site 22)

archaeologists that the place was the remains of a fort, perhaps hastily built pending the completion of the much larger fort nearby.

Here one can turn and retrace the way back to the medieval road, or if continuing southwards and taking the first two turns to the right, one arrives back on the medieval road at right angles, opposite a farmhouse. Here, turn left (westward), and a couple of hundred metres will bring one to the top of a hill. The scenery all along the old road is very striking, but on the top of this hill it reaches its zenith overlooking Adrigole Harbour, Bere Island and the open ocean, with the ice-scored shape of Hungry Hill towering in front of us and the road plunging down from Massmount Cross into the gloomy and awe-inspiring glacial valley of Glenlough.

Here the road passes through unfenced commons land until, close to the ruins of Massmount Church, stone walling starts again on the southern side of the road. Shortly before the stone wall there is a standing stone on the south side of the road alongside which a rough track runs southwards. This gradually curves eastward (left) and then takes a sharp bend to the south (right). A smooth piece of rock outcrop runs parallel to the track within the bend and on it is inscribed a circle-enclosed cross, 14 cm in diameter and formed by using a compass set at a radius of 7 cm to scribe four arcs that intersect at the centre of the primary circle. Apparently it was intended to form a marigold pattern but the craftsman bungled his job. About 300m due south there is a similar, but less elaborate cross, which is more clearly inscribed but is much more difficult to find. [1]

These crosses are similar to some used as dedication crosses on the lintel of church doors but they would appear to be the only examples known on rock outcrops and there has been much discussion as to their purpose. A popular suggestion is that they were used for astronomical purposes. It has also been suggested that the rocks on which they appear may have been used as altars and in the case of the first cross this is quite possible, but less likely in the case of the second. That eminent authority on early Christianity, the late Professor Hodie, believed them to be preaching crosses, where the early monks taught Christianity, but his brother-in-law, Sir Thomas Kendricks, maintained that they were too small, to which Professor Hodie retorted that these crosses *were* small so as not to attract those who were against the new religion. Associated with this may be the tradition that the tribe of Corca Luidhe, or Dairine (O'Driscolls), who in early times occupied all the land from Kenmare Bay to Cork Harbour, were said to be the first to have taught Christianity in Ireland.

Another possible explanation for these crosses is that they may have marked the bounds of tarmon lands, that is, lands handed over to the church for its support, a view strengthened by the fact that two local people have described similar crosses, but the descriptions do not quite tally with the crosses already found, so there may be at least one or possibly two more crosses to be discovered. Yet another explanation is that they may have been moulds for making the communion hosts, for in the early church the host was about five or six inches (13-15cm) in diameter and was brought up to the altar by members of the congregation and presented to the priest who blessed it, broke it up and presented it to the communicants. A local family did have the duty of making, in recent years, the communion hosts and the mould for this purpose was kept in their house nearby, but this is almost certainly purely coincidental. Nor, traditionally, do the crosses appear to have any connection with the holy well of St. Mochuda 250m or so to the west of Cross No. 2.

Before leaving this area there are a couple more points of interest. From just below where the track turns sharply south, near the first cross, a long line of large boulders stretches southwards and near the commencement of this line, to the west of it, is a standing stone. It may have marked a tribal boundary, a view supported by the presence to the east of this line of boulders of a very much ruined ring fort. Scanty though the remains are, they are of considerable interest in showing how these forts were built. Although all the superstructure has vanished, the circle, through which runs a modern wall, may clearly be seen. What one now sees is, basically, a ground plan of the fort. The circular embankment was first formed by placing standing stones and large boulders to form a circle and on to this were added smaller stones, rocks and earth to a height of about 4m. Within the circle near the modern wall, a parallel double line of small stones runs from the perimeter to the centre of the circle, and this undoubtedly marked the entrance to the souterrain, or underground chamber. The fort is built in a very exposed position which, no doubt, accounts for it having been so badly eroded. There is another fort due south, with the embankment remaining, but the fosse has been completely removed, presumably for farming requirements. It is of little interest, except as proofs of population.

Back to the ruins of Massmount Church: this is a post-penal days church, probably successor to the old church of Kilcaskan. It went out of use little over 100 years ago and is not of great interest. From Massmount Cross, below to the left there is a circular patch of very green grass and outside its perimeter is a small standing stone, almost certainly the site of a completely destroyed circle of standing stones. Further evidence is a large cup-marked boulder on the roadside by this circular patch. Cup-marks are small artificial depressions about 25-100 mm in diameter. They occur in groups of five, seven, nine or eleven and invariably mark the site of a burial, and it is not surprising to find a boulder so marked within a circle of standing stones.

At the bottom of the hill a lane runs to the right in to a farmhouse and the road turns sharp left. Around the next bend one comes to a junction left. A stile opposite leads into a circular field containing a boulder burial and immediately behind there is a standing stone next to a holly tree. The field is completely surrounded by holly trees, the sacred tree of the druids, and there is another small standing stone in it. A few hundred metres further on the road joins the main Glengarriff to Castletownbere road.

Back at Massmount Cross one road leads north into the gloomy vale of Glenlough and the other goes south to join, about 1.5 km down, the main road, opposite Adrigole Church at Drumlave. Both are of equal interest. From the crossroads one can see to the left, and on the western side of the road, some standing stones. They would seem to be the remnants of a destroyed circle of standing stones with an outlier, that is, a standing stone outside the circle. To the south, right beside them, may be found a wigwam-type hut foundation and a medieval house site, of the sort with two doors directly opposite each other on each side of the fireplace.

In the adjoining field to the southwest is another megalithic site, which is marked on the Ordnance Survey six inch map as a 'stone circle'. However, it is very small and the stones stand edge to edge, which is very unusual for circles of standing stones. It might be a hut site but seems too small and, moreover, the floor consists of fairly large stones and is very rough. It has been suggested that it might have been a place for dipping sheep but the rough floor is against this idea. Several people who have a good knowledge of burial cairns have proposed that it may be the remains of one and this would seem the most likely suggestion were it not for the fact that such megalithic monuments have not previously been found in this area.

Continuing down the road to Drumlave, before fencing begins on the road side, in the valley to the right just by a stone fence will be found a good example of a circular hut site and nearby a possible 'wigwam' site.

Go on down the Drumlave road, pass two entrance laneways to the left, enter the first field on the eastern side of the road and in the next field will be found a much ruined and overgrown fort, but one that is interesting because the inward-facing bank of the remains of the fosse is lined with boulders, an unusual feature. In the field on the opposite side of the road to the church at Drumlave there is a small standing stone.

Northwards from Massmount Cross into the valley of Glenlough, passing a section of unfenced road, one comes to a place, about 500m in from Massmount Cross, where the road drops down between high banks. Here, to the left side of the road a 'caher' is marked on the Ordnance Survey map. A caher is a stone fort, usually circular, whereas this is a semi-circular stone enclosure, with a pile of stones at one end, which looks very much like a court cairn, that is, a burial chamber with an open court, possibly for some form of ceremony. Expert friends in that field of archaeology claim that it is a court cairn but, again, such megaliths are not known so far south. Another 500m or so further on, above the road on the righthand side will be seen a large standing stone. A local man claims that this is the remaining one of a circle of standing stones and in support of this claim, hollows or pot-holes where other stones probably stood have been found here.

The road continues up the valley, turning sharply left to cross the Adrigole River. The old road from Castletownbere to Cork ran up here to the narrowest point of the Adrigole River, where it could easily be bridged by a couple of large flagstones, and making use, on the way, of the excellent ford at Inchintaglin to cross the Clashduv River. Soon after crossing the river the road again turns sharply left in front of a small standing stone, probably a megalithic signpost.

A short distance brings one to the monastic complex of Kilcaskan, which appears on the Ordnance Survey six inch map as 'Kilcascan Church (in ruins)', 'graveyard', 'Toberatemple' and 'Monumental pillar'. The See of Ross, in which this area is, was founded by St. Fachnan about the year 570, but there seems little or no reference to Kilcaskan until much later. The present ruins of the church would appear to date from about 900-1000 A.D. but the original buildings would have been built of wood, and in the adjoining field to the northeast of the graveyard may be discerned various mounds and hollows, apparently the foundations of wooden buildings, and indeed it does not take much imagination to visualize the site of a mill here. In the top northeastern corner of the field is a circular stone enclosure and it is obvious the settlement was quite a large one. It does not appear in the Decretal Letter of Pope Innocent III, but it does appear in a Taxation Roll of Pope Nicholas (1277-1280), as 'Ecca de Kylkascan and Drumfegna Imr'. Glengarriff, Adrigole and Bunane, the last named being on the northern side of the road from Glengarriff to Kenmare, are in this parish.

There was a little single-roomed hut at Bunane and the priest used to ride over the mountain on Saturdays, hear confessions and stay overnight in the hut to celebrate Mass on Sunday. A story is told that on one occasion both parish priest and curate went over and after they had retired to bed the priest kicked the curate out of the bed three times and after the third time the curate took the horse and rode off home, leaving the priest to fare for himself as well as he could. It is not recorded what

Ogham Stone, Kilcaskan (site 18)

the priest said to the curate when he got back!

The monumental pillar is in the graveyard and, though some have described it as a representation of the rising sun, it is in fact an ogham stone, the top of which has been broken off, thus rendering it unreadable.

In Kilcaskan Church there used to be, within living memory, a stone about the size and shape of a skull which people would rub around their foreheads to cure headaches and here there may be an association with the Scottish St. Fillan. At Dochart Bridge at Killin in Perthshire is St. Fillan's Mill where there is a collection of stones of differing shapes that were used to cure pains by rubbing the affected part with the suitably shaped stone. One of these stones was shaped like a skull and was used for curing headaches.[2]   I have been told that Cascan is the Irish Gaelic version of the Scottish Gaelic Fillan. However, Charles Smith says: 'in Bantry Bay there is still a place called Ardragoal, probably named from a clan of the Gauls or Celtiberi, who landed here. Ardgoal or Ardgyle is the same name. A colony of the Clan of Gaul, or Celtiberi, sailed over from Ireland to the Western Isles and gave the country of Argyle, in Scotland, their name.'[3]

As regards 'Toberatemple': east of the graveyard, on the opposite of the road, just around the corner there is a small gate and inside immediately to the right under bushes is the holy well. It is a bullaun-like hollow, through which water seeps, on rock outcrop. Alongside it a crude cross has been cut, apparently over the centuries, by people making the sign of the cross with a stone. From here down to the nearby river curves a line of boulders, called in Sweden a 'processional way', and it would seem to have been a place where the druids brought water up from the river to the bullaun (round hollow in a stone) for worship. Then St. Cascan arrived, Christianized the well with the sign of Christ, and probably, as was usual with the early missioners, used it for baptismal purposes. It must be one of the oldest places of worship in the country and it is a pity that it is not more accessible for the passing

32

tourist to see.

The following are the oldest readable monumental inscriptions in Kilcaskan graveyard. The first memorial slab is within the walls of the church.

'Here lies the bodies of Florence O'Sullivan and Catherine O'Sullivan. The former departed this life on Easter Sunday April 16 1797 aged 81 years, the latter on March 2 1798 aged 74'.

'Erected in memory of Henery Trenwith Esq died 7ber ye 9th 1807 in the 27th year of his life'
'This monument is erected in memory of Edward Trenwith Esq who died 7ber ye 29th 1811 in the 31st year of his life.'

Trenwith memorial slab, Kilcaskan

These two Trenwith memorial slabs are the best cut in the barony and bear some floral decoration.

Continuing from Kilcaskan graveyard, a couple of bends in the road bring us to Inchintaglin Bridge, a rather graceful structure curving across the river over a clear pool which makes an excellent swimming place. Before the building of the bridge there was a ford here, bringing the Castletownbere-Cork road across the river and a glance at the northern side of the bridge will show what an excellent place it was for a ford, the river being wide, shallow and running over a smooth rock ledge. A little further on, where the road bends to the left and climbs up to come out on the Healy Pass road, a rough track may be observed on the righthand side of the road. This is a remnant of the old medieval road.

On coming out on the Healy Pass road turn left, towards the sea. Many people stop at the grotto here but I wonder how many notice the fine gallaun, or standing stone, above the eastern bank of the river. It is an impressive one, but it is two fields beyond the river and in summer is concealed by foliage so it is not easy to see. Opposite the Glenbrook Bar, on the eastern bank of the river will be seen a megalithic tomb, marked on the Ordnance Survey six inch map as a 'cromlech'. It may be reached from the Cork road, and is rather unusual, consisting of five large standing stones, standing close together and forming a small enclosure.

A short distance away lies a large flat stone which could be the capstone one would expect on such a monument, but it does seem to be too large and, moreover, too far away to have fallen off the standing stones. Against this there is a local traditional tale that a farmer here put up a travelling woman for a night and in the morning she described this monument and asked if there was anything like it around as she had dreamed that there was a box of gold buried there. The local landlord, an O'Sullivan who lived on the other side of Adrigole Harbour at Reen Lodge, ordered his workmen to throw the stones down and dig the place up but none of them would touch it. So he found the local drunkard and gave him a bottle of whiskey with the promise of another when he had the place dug up. Perhaps the first bottle was a mistake and his hand not too steady, for when the man started work the large stone on top fell and killed him and, needless to say, after that everybody was even more reluctant to touch the place. Of course, if he had succeeded in the dig, the most that would have been found would be an urn containing ashes!

Just beyond the Glenbrook Bar a lane to the right leads from the road to the former Church of Ireland graveyard and ruined church. Here is the burial place of Katherine Ellen Puxley, whose memorial inscription reads:

'Sacred to the memory of Katherine the beloved wife of Henry Lavallin Puxley, of Dunboy Castle, who departed this life July 19, 1872, aged 36 years. Blessed are the dead which die in the Lord From henceforth yea Saith the Spirit that they May rest from their labours.

Revelations X1V 13'

She was Katherine Ellen Waller, daughter of Rev. William Waller, Castletown, Co. Limerick and she married Henry Lavallin Puxley of Dunboy Castle. His second wife was Adeline, widow of Colonel William Ferguson Hutchinson. This Katherine Ellen Puxley is said to be the original of Katherine Brodrick and Adeline Ferguson Hutchinson the original of Adeline Price, widow of General Price, in the novel *Hungry Hill* by Daphne du Maurier.

Towards the western end of the village, near the last bend will be seen a small standing stone on a hill to the right of the road. It is opposite a gap in the hills to the west and it is said that in the valley between is a field known as 'the fort field', obvious evidence for these small standing stones being route marks. In this valley there is a large rock known as 'the rock of Gibraltar'.

This is a place of many small streams and can be quite spectacular in wet weather. West of the village, at Reen Bridge, a road goes westerly and another northwesterly, on each side of the river up to the foot of the mountains, both running to near the base of the Mare's Tail waterfall dropping steeply down the side of Hungry Hill. About 1.5 km up the road to the west of the river, where a small quarry makes a convenient turning place, there in a fence on the eastern side of the road is a very impressive large standing stone. Nearby there is a large slab set on edge in the fence, which is probably the remains of a wedge grave. The large, flat slabs of rock used in making these wedge graves were very suitable for making bridges across streams and were often removed for that purpose and, in at least one case, for a mantlepiece!

It is surprising that none of the many tourists who visited the Mare's Tail in the 17th and 19th centuries made any mention of this standing stone, so, it would appear, they must usually have gone up the road on the eastern side of the river. Among the visitors to the Mare's Tail waterfall were circa 1750 Charles Smith, the Cork historian; in 1700 Bishop Dive Downes during a visitation of his diocese; in 1758 that indefatigable traveller, Bishop Pococke; in 1796 the Breton Royalist officer and fugitive from France, de Latocnaye; in 1810 Rev. Horatio Townsend, during the process of compiling his *Statistical Survey of Co. Cork*; Samuel Lewis, for his *Topographical History of Ireland* 1837; and in 1848, the English Poet Laureate, Alfred Lord Tennyson.

Few people look at things from the same viewpoint and these half dozen or so travellers were no exception. Charles Smith says, 'Not far from Ross Mac Owen is one of the largest and highest waterfalls in this kingdom. The cataract is very visible from the town of Bantry, at least fourteen miles distant from it'[4] and goes on to give a very precise and exact description of all its twists and turns as it bounds from rock to rock down to the sea. Dive Downes merely refers to a river running down a steep side of the hill. The other bishop, Pococke – who was born in Southampton in 1704 and took his degree as doctor of laws at Christ Church, Oxford in 1733, after which he travelled extensively, being in the east from 1737 to 1742 – describes the waterfall more comprehensively.

We came to Adrigole to see the famous waterfall, which has been so much spoken of and is to the West. When we first saw it, it appeared like a vein of sparr in the rocky mountains. We walked about two miles to it. The whole mountain is call'd "Hungry Hill", the top of which is computed to be 700 yards above the sea, but I do not think it so much, the upper part is very steep, it may be about one third of the height; at the foot of this eminence is a lake on that part of the mountain call'd Coumgira (the crooked leg).

He goes on to describe the course of the fall and its various deviations and to comment on the beauty of the scene. He also mentions an echo there which he compares with that near Milan and speaks of a fall to the north called Eskimileen (poet's hillock) and another to the south called Garavileen (rough island).[5]

In 1796 de Latocnaye says, 'Between Glengariff and Bear haven is seen a very high cascade, of nearly perpendicular fall, from a mountain which has got the name of "Hungry Hill," and not without reason.'[6] Rev. Horatio Townsend writes of this 'grand and singular spectacle .... in comparison with which O'Sullivan's Cascade at Killarney and the waterfall at Powerscourt near Dublin, shrink into insignificance.'[7]

Alfred Lord Tennyson visited Ireland three times, in 1842, 1848 and 1878. The Irish poet Aubrey de Vere and Tennyson first met when de Vere was on a visit to his uncle, Lord Limerick, in London in 1842 and they remained close friends until Tennyson's death in 1893. In 1848 Tennyson stayed with de Vere at his home, Curraghchase, Adare, Co. Limerick, and also visited the Knight of Kerry at Valentia, from where he drove over to see the waterfall on Hungry Hill. Unfortunately, the rain was so heavy they could not see the waterfall and had to take shelter in a wayside cottage. However, the trip was not wasted as Tennyson was interested in the Irish character and greatly impressed by their car driver, an O'Sullivan, who claimed to be closely related to the families of MacCarthy More and O'Sullivan Beare, in evidence of which he produced a ponderous seal containing their arms quartered together. Tennyson thought the man looked every inch a chief and was quite ready to believe him. Tennyson gave a sixpence to a little boy in the cabin where they had sheltered and was astonished at the volubility of the gratitude which the child's mother showed, and felt rather ashamed for not having given more, but his driver said her gratitude was because the child's hand had been crossed with silver by the dark stranger, which was considered lucky.

The Ordnance Survey six inch maps of this area show, on the bare hills above Adrigole, three 'cromlechs'. Being on bare rock this seems an unlikely place for burials, but the only one of these that I have inspected has all the requirements of a 'cloghogle', or 'raised stone', that is, a large boulder resting on three smaller rocks. The chamber thus formed would be too small to allow for an inhumation, but, possibly, there may have been a cremated burial, the ashes being placed in a small urn. In such a case one would expect the burial chamber to have been covered with a mound of earth or stones, yet many of these 'cloghogles' are on rock outcrop, often sharply sloping, so it would seem that if a mound of earth were erected over them it would have been rapidly eroded. There are in a field overlooking Castletownbere four of these 'raised stones', but in this case it would have been feasible for them to have been covered by a mound of stones or earth.

Returning to Reen Bridge and continuing westward for a 1.5 km, where the road begins to climb Derreeny Hill a little road runs to the left down to Derreeny pier. This makes a nice picnicking place or at high tide a good place for swimming, but the beach is stony.

Climbing Derreeny Hill, a little after the road straightens out, will be seen, on the right, a deep crevice running up the mountain side. West of and below this is the tiny townland of Keamnalicky, only 7 acres 3 roods and 21 perches in area. Here on the Ordnance Survey six inch map is marked an antiquity, 'Darriheendermot'. Extensive searches in this small area have failed to produce anything of a megalithic nature and the antiquity probably refers to an oak tree upon which one Diarmaid O'Donovan was hanged in 1581; the withered tree trunk is said to remain still.

In December 1581 a Captain Zouche (so spelt by Connellan in his edition of the *Annals of the Four Masters* but in Donovan's edition spelt 'Suitsi') was stirring up the tribes of the south of Ireland against each other and in this month he came from Cork, through Carbery, to the monastery of Bantry where he collected the MacSweenys, the O'Donovans and a number of the chiefs and of the gentlemen of Carbery and sent them to raid Beara, where they took much plunder and booty.

Donal Cam O'Sullivan Beare was quite young and his estate was still in the hands of the tanist (successor apparent), Owen O'Sullivan Beare. (Donal Cam was described by Don Philip O'Sullivan Beare, the historian, in his account of this action as being 'adolescent' and Owen O'Sullivan Beare was being held prisoner by the English in Limerick). Young Donal Cam was loathe to see all his property seized and borne away without any resistance, so he gathered some of his friends and relations, not much more than 50 in number, and gave chase.

The principal man of the O'Sullivans here then would appear to have been Reiry O'Sullivan Beare of Barness. Now Reiry was a coward and lazy and, like many such, a braggart also. He told them he was not ready yet but that he would overtake them on the way and kill more men than anybody else in that little band. Donal Cam and his few followers overtook the men of Carbery at *Laitheach na Damh* (slough of the oxen), near Darriheendermot, and inflicted a crushing defeat on them, killing almost 300, including Diarmaid O'Donovan. The local account says Diarmaid O'Donovan was hanged on the branch of an oak tree but the *Annals of the Four Masters* say he was buried under an oak tree.[8]

Like Admiral Herbert, Reiry O'Sullivan Beare was good at avoiding battles and he arrived when all was over, protesting that they should have waited for him to arrive before they commenced battle and boasting of all he would have killed if he had been in time.

Donal Cam pointed out a dead man lying on his gun and told Reiry to bring him the weapon. Reiry very nervously made his way over to the corpse and asked, 'Please, sir, would you give me the gun.' Naturally there was no reply and Reiry went back to Donal Cam and said, 'He wouldn't give it.' Donal then told a young teenager standing nearby to get it and the boy ran over, kicked away the body and grabbed the gun!

Before getting too far away from Adrigole it may be of interest to note that in 1962 the wife of the then Spanish ambassador to Ireland, Señor Baraibar, said her ancestors, named Bermingham, came from Adrigole, near Bantry, from where they left in the middle of the 18th century to settle at San Sebastian in northern Spain. A Thomas Bermingham was elected mayor, and in the old part of the city is a square called Plaza de Alcalde Bermingham named after him. A priest called Patricio Bermingham, born in Galway, was one of the sponsors for Patricio Terry of Madrid when Terry was appointed Knight of Santiago in 1702 and Raimundo Bermingham, a captain in the Spanish service, who was born in the diocese of Tuam, was sponsor for Juan O'Brien of Madrid in 1752.

SKETCH-MAP OF CASTLETOWNBERE AREA AND BERE ISLAND

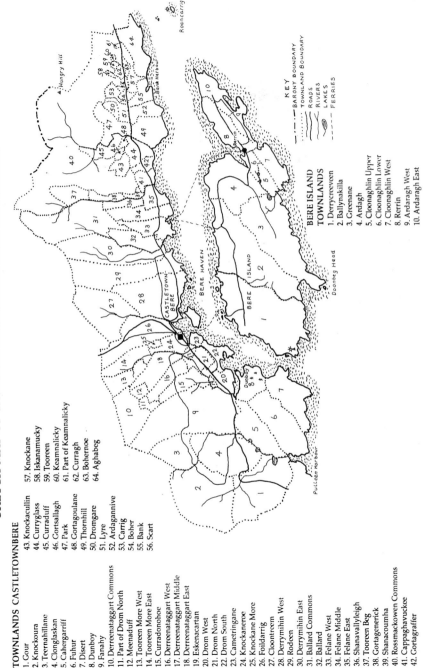

TOWNLANDS CASTLETOWNBERE

1. Gour
2. Knockoura
3. Teernahillane
4. Clonglaskan
5. Cahergarriff
6. Fuhur
7. Disert
8. Dunboy
9. Fanahy
10. Derreenataggart Commons
11. Part of Drom North
12. Meenaduff
13. Tooreen More West
14. Tooreen More East
15. Curradonohoe
16. Derreenataggart West
17. Derreenataggart Middle
18. Derreenataggart East
19. Eskenacartan
20. Drom West
21. Drom North
22. Drom South
23. Cametringane
24. Knockaneroe
25. Knockane More
26. Foildarrig
27. Cloontreem
28. Derrymihin West
29. Rodeen
30. Derrymihin East
31. Ballard Commons
32. Ballard
33. Felane West
34. Felane Middle
35. Felane East
36. Shanavallyleigh
37. Tooreen Beg
38. Gortagemerick
39. Shanacoumha
40. Rossmackowen Commons
41. Cappaghavuckee
42. Gortagraffer

43. Knockacullin
44. Curryglass
45. Curraduff
46. Gortsallagh
47. Park
48. Gortagoulane
49. Thornhill
50. Dromgare
51. Lyre
52. Ardagannive
53. Carrig
54. Boher
55. Bank
56. Scart
57. Knockane
58. Iskanamucky
59. Tooreen
60. Keamnalicky
61. Part of Keamnalicky
62. Curragh
63. Bohernoe
64. Aghabeg

BERE ISLAND TOWNLANDS

1. Derrycreeveen
2. Ballynakilla
3. Greenane
4. Ardagh
5. Cloonaghlin Upper
6. Cloonaghlin Lower
7. Cloonaghlin West
8. Rerrin
9. Ardaragh West
10. Ardaragh East

39

Chapter 4

Jacques Fontaine

The next seaward-running road just west of Keamnalicky leads down to Ahabeg where there is a small sheltered harbour, pleasant for swimming or picnicking, but which dries out at low water. It is protected from the open sea by a jagged reef running parallel to the shore. Outside this reef the water is of exceptional depth and some years ago there was talk of it being developed for building oil rigs.

The next harbour along the coast to the west is Bank, where, in the early 18th century, there were attempts at industrial development but which, mainly through the uncertainty of the times, fell through after a few years. The founder of this development was a Huguenot, Jacques Fontaine, who had fled from France at the time of the persecution of the Protestants, and after many adventures landed at Appledore in the Bristol Channel near Barnstaple in December 1685.[1]   He was received kindly by a man of Barnstaple who was worth £10,000 and his sister who had a fortune of £3,000. Unfortunately this good lady decided she would like to marry Fontaine and, as a kind of compensation, suggested that her brother should marry Fontaine's fiancée. The proposal found favour with none of the parties concerned except the lady herself, and Fontaine and his fiancée lost no time in getting married, in February 1686. Fontaine's wife was a Boursiquot, from which family was later descended the famous Irish actor and playwright Dion Boucicault; through this connection I first found Fontaine.

Fontaine and his wife met many vicissitudes in England, some of them to him surprising, such as when he was made a grant of £30 as a distressed Protestant and found that before receiving it he would have to certify he had received communion according to the rites of the Anglican church. He had regularly received communion in the Anglican church but flatly refused to do so in order to obtain charity. Another shock was being accused of being a Jesuit in disguise!

Fontaine gradually built up good businesses in various spheres, teaching, as a shopkeeper and eventually as a manufacturer of various kinds of cloth he had himself invented, but he attracted a lot of opposition and was obviously not a man who could hold an interest in one occupation for long, so in 1694 he decided to sell his shop, which he did profitably, and seek employment as a minister to a French church.

Fontaine came to Dublin and was recommended to Cork. Returning to Taunton, he closed down his manufactory and made all arrangements for transfer to Cork, where he arrived on 24 December 1694 and assumed his pastoral duties on 19 January 1695. These pastoral duties carried with them no remuneration, so, to support his family, he took a large house about five miles (8 km) southeast of Cork at a place since known as Fountainstown (or Fontainestown), and there, once more, set up a manufactory of a good quality broadcloth, which proved successful.

When he came to Cork first he was allowed to preach at Christ Church, after the English services were over; later they used the county court room for the French services and finally Fontaine arranged a room in the ground floor of his house as a church.

Another son was born to his wife in September 1697 and he stated that he was now at the height of his ambition, but if he had reached the zenith the nadir was soon to come. Fontaine chose an unfortunately appropriate time to preach a sermon on dishonesty, unaware that two important members of his congregation intended quietly slipping out of Cork with a cargo for which they had not paid, and could not pay, on that very morning. This led to a split in his congregation and in June 1698 he parted with them.

In July he foolishly accepted a cargo consigned to him by a Frenchman he did not know and he paid the freight and duty on this, but when the wine, which comprised the major portion of the cargo, was tested it proved so inferior that the dealers would only pay £1 per hogshead for what he had paid a duty of £3 per hogshead. A second cargo caused him another, though not so grievous loss. On top of this the English government passed an Act of Parliament prohibiting the export of manufactured woollen goods from Ireland. This, of course, ruined his woollen manufactory.

Fontaine had thought of taking up farming but it was ill-advisedly suggested that he should combine this with fishing and it would seem that the idea was that while the apostles, who from fishermen became preachers, he, who had been a preacher, would become a fisherman! He sought advice, and purchased secondhand tackle, boats and equipment from Colonel Beecher at Baltimore and Colonel Townsend at Castlehaven. He then went to Beara and hired a considerable farm from Mr. Boyd at £100 per annum, another from Mr. Davis at £31 10s and a third at £18. In this new undertaking he went into partnership with his cousin, John Arnauld, and Messrs. Renue, Thomas and Gourbould, all merchants in London. This was a mistake, for Fountaine was not a man who could work with others. As they had not yet started fishing they chartered their boat the *Robert* to a merchant in Cork to go to Spain for a cargo of salt, oranges and lemons, but the captain, James Joy, ran the vessel ashore on the French coast and sold both it, which was little damaged, and the cargo and settled down in France.

In May 1700 they first began fishing for cod off Dursey Island, but the weather was bad and the fish scarce and, to be brief, Fontaine's stay in Beara during the next eight years or so was a tale of misfortune after misfortune. The fishing so badly failing, they tried using their surplus boats for trading voyages to Virginia, Spain, Madeira and the Barbadoes, but few of these proved profitable.

It must have been particularly galling that the end of a good fishing season should have coincided with arrival in Berehaven during the month of August 1701 of their vessel the *Goodwill*, packed with a valuable cargo of tobacco. Fontaine had, in this season, cured over 200,000 herrings, pressed enough to fill 200 hogsheads and also had 200 barrels of pickled herrings. He also had 12 tierces (a tierce is one third of a pipe and a pipe was usually 105 gallons) of salmon, 700 or 800 dried codfish, and 2,000 flukes, altogether worth about £1,200, all ready to be shipped off to Leghorn in Italy. But the *Goodwill* had first to go to London to discharge her cargo of tobacco.

Now there were at this time rumours of war with Spain, and Fontaine's partners in London owned a large quantity of wine which was stored in Spain, so, as soon as she was unloaded, they dispatched the *Goodwill* there to collect the wine and, while the ship kept shuttling to and fro between England and Spain, Fontaine bombarded his partners urging them to send back the *Goodwill* or dispatch another vessel in her place, but to them the wine was all that was worth considering and they told Fontaine to sell the fish locally for what he could get.

There was a vessel loading at Berehaven for Leghorn and Fontaine managed to send a small quantity of each kind of fish by this, and, judging by what he sold these for, he would have got £1,500 for his whole stock of fish, if only he had the *Goodwill* to take them. Eventually his partners sent him a boat, a leaky old vessel in need of repairs, which did not arrive in Berehaven until January 1702. She was loaded as quickly as possible and set sail for Leghorn on 5 February, but only got as far as the mouth of the harbour, where she sprang a leak. Eventually, after the leak was repaired she got away to Leghorn, where all the fish was sold, but by now most of the fish had gone bad and what money they got for them was scarcely enough to cover expenses. At this point, no doubt impelled by Fontaine's importunities, his London partners decided to get out of such a losing concern, though the losses were mainly due to their withholding the *Goodwill*. They maintained that Fontaine owed them £600 and, once again, he found himself utterly ruined.

Fontaine was a Justice of Peace, and did all he could to stop smuggling, a proceeding which made him unpopular with everybody, both Protestant and Catholic liking their uncustomed wine. Fontaine mentions in his diary that there were not more than half a dozen

Protestants in the adjacent country besides his own family. Dive Downes in his 'Visitation of His Diocese' notes that 'in the whole parish of Killaconenagh (Berehaven) there are about 15 Protestant families, 5 French, 5 Scotch Dissenters and 5 English Conformists.'[2]

Fontaine gave jobs to 13 destitute Frenchmen, but they rapidly became discouraged and left, so it would appear that not only was he constantly at loggerheads with his Irish neighbours, both Protestant and Catholic, but also with French privateers raiding the coast, with his partners, and even with the English government both in England and in Dublin. When his Boucicault descendant visited me here he very kindly presented me with a copy of Fontaine's biography and one morning, at breakfast, I remarked that I had always had the greatest sympathy with poor old Fontaine but after reading his biography I had lost all this for I did not believe that any man could have fought with so many people and have *always* been in the right!

On 1 June 1704 at eight o'clock in the morning Fontaine's house at Bank was attacked by a French privateer, an attack which lasted until four o'clock in the afternoon and which the little garrison successfully repulsed. Fontaine immediately wrote a full account of the incident to Lord Cox, then Lord Chancellor of Ireland, and to the Duke of Ormond, the Lord Lieutenant. He then built some fortifications to the back of his house and, to the front, facing the entrance to the creek, he raised a rampart of turf 18 feet (5.5m) in thickness, since when the place has been known as 'the sod fort'. Fontaine's house was only taken down in the 1920s when the stones were taken to rebuild houses burned by the 'Black and Tans'. An old man told me that when he was a boy the house was still high enough for it to be considered quite a feat to throw a stone over it.

From various remarks made by Fontaine it is possible to visualize the type of settlement he had at Bank. He mentions a 'garret window' and 'dormer windows' so his residence would appear to have been similar to the style of house still in use around here. We know he added fortifications to the back of his house and these probably included the tower which he refers to in his account of the second attack, where he also mentions 'the gates of the large court in front'.

The second attack by a French privateer took place on 8 October 1708 and found Fontaine much less prepared, at least as far as his garrison was concerned, for this now consisted of his wife and himself, their children and four servants, two of whom were mere cow boys and the other two had never seen battle. Much of Fontaine's account of the preliminaries to this attack must be considered conjectural, but his account of the actual attack would appear to be factual and in this he says, 'Their first act was to set fire to the malthouse, which was towards

Bank Harbour & Hungry Hill

the east, then to the stacks of straw, hay and grain, which were at the north and east, and after that to the cow-house, stable, and long fish-press, which were to the west of my house.' In fact the fish-press (local name, 'palace') would appear to have been just to the southeast of his house, but it is obvious he had quite a substantial holding. All the smoke prevented them from seeing the enemy properly and Fontaine himself was injured when his musket burst, breaking three of his ribs and his right collarbone and badly tearing the skin of his right hand. Eventually the French breached the walls and Fontaine was forced to surrender under terms.

Much of his account now consists of recriminations, protesting that the French had broken the terms of the surrender by stealing all his loose property and taking him prisoner, but all to no avail and he was carried off. His wife, who appears to have been an indomitable person, followed the boat out to Dursey Sound where she managed to make contact and arranged to ransom her husband for £100, the privateer agreeing to wait off Dursey Island until she had the money collected. She was unable to raise more than £30, which she borrowed from their landlord Captain Boyd. She returned to Dursey Sound with her son Peter, several of their tenants and a friend, Mr. Hutchins of Berehaven.

Eventually the French agreed to release her husband on payment of the £30, provided one of their sons replaced his father as security for the further payment of the £70. That night, Tuesday 11 October, Fontaine slept in the house of Mr. Hutchins at Berehaven and the next day went to Bantry where his wife waited until she saw him in the care of a good French surgeon and then she went on to Cork to collect the balance of the ransom money. She borrowed £20 from the bishop and could easily have borrowed the balance from her friends but the Cork merchants urged her not to pay any more as her son would be released when the privateer got back to France, and she accepted their advice.

Sure enough, when the privateer got back to St. Malo, the governor of Brest was very indignant with the captain for having taken a hostage at a time when England and France were at peace; he refused to allow Peter Fontaine to be landed and the captain had to take him on the privateer's next cruise.

Meanwhile, when the commanding officers of Kinsale and Plymouth heard of this, they placed into irons all the French prisoners in these two places. So when the privateer arrived back for the second time at St. Malo he found an extremely indignant governor of Brest who ordered the captain, under pain of death or imprisonment, to return Peter to the place from where he had taken him, and that without payment of ransom, and so young Peter was restored to his family.

Now, apparently, Fontaine decided on a more peaceful course in life, so he disposed of all his Beara interests and opened a school in Dublin, admitted by himself to be a fairly severe one, but it was successful and he continued it until September 1721 when ill health caused him to close it down and retire, his wife having died in January of that year.

Fontaine resembled Dickens's character Uriah Heep, in that he frequently professed to be a humble man; and yet his humility was constantly swamped by his arrogance! He declared that his name was really De la Fontaine but he could not bring himself to use such an aristocratic title. In fact, under then French law he could not legally have indulged in commerce if he had retained his title. At one point after the first siege of his settlement, when he was looking, successfully, for compensation and a pension, he wrote: 'My inventive genius had now entirely forsaken me.' Certainly he did have many successes against considerable odds, but one wonders how much was due to his wife who seems to have been a self-effacing person who showed an admirably efficient strength of mind and placidity of character, especially in the two sieges.

Of their family, John, a half-pay officer, went to Virginia where he purchased a plantation. His brother Peter was ordained for the British colonies and joined him in Virginia. John returned to London from Virginia in July 1719 and eventually became a watchmaker. Moses had been studying law but had some scruples against it and became an engraver. Francis, who had taken his degree of Master of Arts and was well skilled in Oriental languages, took Holy Orders and settled at St.

Margaret's parish, King William County, Virginia, having married in London Miss Mary Glanisson.

In November 1713 Captain Boulay, a Frenchman and cavalry officer on half pay, called on Fontaine, with whom he had no previous acquaintance, and said he was now over 80 years old and wished to make provision for his only charge, his 13-year-old granddaughter, Elizabeth Fourreau. Having heard much of the good qualities of the Fontaine family, he said he would like her to marry one of them, so Fontaine suggested that she should come as a boarder in his school, in order to give his sons a chance of deciding which liked her most. Within a few months it was decided that Peter was the one she should marry and they were duly married on 29 March 1714, before Peter had taken his degree of Bachelor of Arts. In March 1715 Captain Boulay died, leaving Peter £1,000. He had now taken his degree and on his ordination his wife accompanied Peter to Virginia.

On 20 October 1716 Fontaine's daughter, Mary Anne, married Matthew Maury of Castel Mauron, Gascony, a French refugee, according to his father-in-law, 'a very honest man and a good economist, but without property'. He and his wife and son settled in Virginia in 1719.

As a child Fontaine met with an accident which rendered him lame for life. Following the death of his wife in 1721, he started writing his history of the family on 26 March 1722, when he was 64 years old, and he appears to have died in 1728 when 'James Fontaine, Dublin, Clerk (in Holy Orders)' appears in the *Index to Prerogative Wills of Ireland*.[3] The fact that his will appears in this index meant he must have had property in more than one parish.

Fontaine's original diary was translated from the French by Mrs. Anne Maury and published in New York in 1853 with copious letters and journals written by family members. It was republished, without the letters and journals, by the Religious Tract Society of London.

Another descendant was Matthew Fontaine Maury, the greatest hydrographer in the United States navy, who, on 28 January 1859, read a paper to the Royal Dublin Society in which he foretold the success of the Atlantic marine cable. In Samuel Smile's account, *The Huguenots in England and Ireland* (London: John Murray, 1889), Fontaine's daughter, Mary Anne, married Rev. James Maury, Fredericksville Parish, Louisa County, Virginia, and it was from them that Matthew Fontaine Maury was descended.

Smiles also refers to the settlement of French refugees in Cork congregated in the parish of St. Paul, whose principal street is French Church St.; in this church services were conducted in French until the beginning of the 19th century. Until the arrival of Fontaine the principal settlers in Cork were merchants and traders.

In 1969, when showing a Scottish student around Bank Harbour, we met an American, Rev. Oscar Fontaine, who was on a year's exchange visit to the Wesleyan Church in Cork and he expressed an interest in his ancestor Jacques Fontaine of Bank Harbour. I was able to inform him that I had a cannon ball that had been fired by the French at his ancestor, which I later presented to him.

Prior to this, in 1967, I had a visit from a great-grandson of Dion Boucicault who was also interested in the Fontaine family, and since then I have met descendants of the Fontaines now resident in Wiltshire near Bowood, the ancestral home of the Petty-Fitzmaurices, descendants of Sir William Petty, author of the Down Survey. The Irish seat of these Petty-Fitzmaurices, Lords Lansdowne and Marquesses of Shelburne is Derreen House, Lauragh.

Chapter 5

Prehistory and Early Christianity

The next turn off the main road down to the sea leads to Sandmount. The beach here is very rocky but at low tide there is a sandy strand which makes a very good bathing place for young children as the water is shallow and its depth increases very slowly.

Before leaving the main road, nearly opposite the turn down to Sandmount but a little to the east, is a gate and in a field a few fields from the road (it is difficult to say exactly how many as some of the fields appear to have been enlarged) will be found two small standing stones, one on the north bank of a small stream and the other on the south bank. These are marked on the Ordnance Survey six inch map as 'Gallauns'. They are neatly shaped, almost polished, and for this reason I would consider them to be of the later period of standing stones. Easier access to these might be by walking up the narrow by-road running northwest from the main road. Just beyond the first farmyard about 450m up, one of the stones will be seen in the second field in from the road. Nearby is a very much ruined ring fort, of little interest. Owing to the enlargement of fields, the increase in the height of fences and other general, and very necessary, farm improvements many of these archaeological sites have become difficult of access.

The question is frequently asked as to what these megalithic monuments, standing stones, wedge graves, ring forts and hut sites meant and why were they, often with considerable difficulty, erected at all. Obviously the hut sites, both circular and wigwam, were the habitations of the lower classes. Both types have been in use for a very long time and are often found near a ring fort or medieval house site. The medieval house was oblong, with two doors near one end of the house, opposite to each other, and between them was the open hearth. They were thatched and the smoke escaped through the roof as best it could. These were probably the most common type of house in the country but, being built with mud walls and a thatched roof, once the thatch was gone the walls rapidly returned to earth. Remains of them are often to be found in monastic settlements, where the enclosing walls provided a certain amount of protection.

The ring forts were the habitations of the well-to-do, owners of cattle and, in earlier days, slaves. Their size depended on the wealth of the owners and some of them can be very impressive. To the seaward their defences were very strong, with high, steep banks and a deep fosse, while on the mountain side the defences were often quite weak, so it was apparent that any attacks they might expect would have come from the sea. These ring forts are the most numerous of ancient structures in Ireland; it is believed that there are between 30,000 and 40,000 of them in the country. They vary considerably in size, the diameter of the interior varying from 15m to as much as 60m. They were in use for a very long time. They were known in the Bronze Age (circa 2000 B.C. to 500 B.C.) and Cahermacnaghten in Co. Clare was in use by the O'Davoren family for their famous law school as late as the end of the 17th century, while in others medieval pottery has been found. In the absence of any excavation it would be very difficult to place even an approximate date on the forts of Beara.

Excavation has shown that wedge graves, boulder dolmens and cairns are, as their names indicate, burial places and so too are some standing stones. Most of the burials would have been cremated and the ashes placed in an urn under a boulder dolmen, which would then be covered with a cairn of stones or earth. In the case of such standing stones as proved to be burial places the urn was buried as the base of the standing stone. The smaller standing stones seem to have invariably marked route ways or were guide lines between one fort and the next. Some of the larger standing stones were similarly used, especially where it was necessary for them to be seen from a distance, such as the two in the vicinity of Cromwell's Road. One of these stands in a fence of large boulders and probably marked a clan or tribal boundary.

In many cases, as at Glenbeg on the northern side of the peninsula, two large standing stones stand about 1m apart, forming a portal, perhaps an official entrance between two tribal areas. Circles of standing stones may be taken as being ritualistic. Cremated burials have been found in them but these may be regarded as being of a dedicatory nature. The use of all these megaliths was, to a large extent, individualistic, and it is obvious from the Bible that in early times the larger standing stones were used, not only to mark graves, such as Rachel's, but also as signs of witness. However, in Biblical times the most common use for the larger standing stones (and also cairns) was as altars, and there was an injunction against the shaping of stones so used. Even in parts of Africa today, on the sides of roads through the jungle, there stand at regular distances small gods about the size of our smaller standing stones, and at these the traveller worships, praying for a safe journey to the next.

The following are some Biblical references to megaliths: Genesis 28: 12, 18, 22; 13: 45-46, 51-52; 35: 14-15, 19-20; Joshua 4: 1-3, 22; 24: 26-27; 1 Samuel 7: 12; Leviticus 25: 1.

With Leviticus, the third book of Moses, we are into the Bronze Age and the Ark of the Covenant has been built as the one place of worship, to be followed later by the temple at Jerusalem. Leviticus deals with the explanation and expansion of the Mosiac Law and lists the types of worship no longer permissible. This book is said to have been the principal reason why the Hebrews, in the Babylonian captivity, did not lose their faith completely. But some of the tribes moved westward away from the priestly orders and the influence of the Tabernacle, and St. Augustine records that even in his day the inhabitants of Hippo, in the early fifth century, regarded themselves as Canaanites, though to most other peoples they would have been known as Phoenicians, under which title they may have come to Ireland. The Biblical sources show that, even in their homeland, the Hebrews lapsed from their faith very easily, so it is no surprise to find them now reverted to the ritualistic circles of standing stones, the use of standing stones as altars and the earlier forms of burial. These forms continued up to, and after, the arrival of Christianity and the foundation of the Celtic church.

The Venerable Bede (circa 673 - 735) records that in the year 430, Pope Celestine sent Palladius to be the first bishop to the Christian Scots (that is, the Irish)[1] but it seems highly probable that Christianity had reached Ireland before this from Irish contacts with England and Gaul, as reflected in the strong tradition of the Corca Luidhe and early Christianity.

The best known pre-Patrician saint to have any connection with Beara was St. Ciaran of Saigir. St. Ciaran is reputed to have been of the Osraige tribe on his father's side and of the Corca Luidhe on his mother's side. He was said to be the first-born of the saints of Ireland and that he visited Rome, where he met St. Patrick, who sent him back to Ireland as his precursor. 'Lives' of St. Ciaran are in the *Codex Salmanticensis* and the *Codex Kilkenniensis*. Other sources say he was born in West Cork and went to the Continent to pursue his education, and by the time he returned to Ireland he was already ordained and a bishop. It is said that Ciaran visited Sylvester and Solonius, the two priests left behind when Palladius departed Ireland, and investigated the state of the church there before moving to Saigir, 7.5 km southeast of Birr, where he founded his monastery. Ciaran's mother, Liadan, is said to be buried within a circle of standing stones on Cape Clear. There is still considerable devotion to Ciaran on Cape Clear, even now, and a former curate there told me he could omit saying Mass on St. Patrick's Day and it would scarcely be noticed but for a couple of weeks before March 5, St. Ciaran's Feast, his parishioners would remind him that the day was a Feast day.

O'Driscoll was the principal name amongst the Corca Luidhe and of them O'Huidhrin in his *Topographical Poems* says:

To the race of Luighee along the shore, I now proceed beyond the bounds to pass the tribe is not meet for me but to record the warriors' fame.

O'Driscoll head chief of the land of Corcaluighe, I treat of now, he took possession of the coasts of Cleire, the fittest headland for the princely lord.

O'Driscoll of the wealthy Beara, rules over the lands of the salmon coast, a blue water shore abounding in harbours, exhibiting to view large fleets of wine.[2]

According to the *Book of Munster* the genealogy of O'Driscoll Bearra was:

Diarmuid (Dermot) or Jeremiah or Donal (Daniel): son of Conchur Bhui (Yellow Cornelius), son of Meic Con (son of Con), son of Mortimer, son of Meic Con, son of Tadhg (Timothy), son of Hugh Garbh (Rough Hugh), son of Fothach, son of Fionn, son of Meic Con, son of Fothach, son of Eidirsgeoil.

In the same book will be found genealogies of other branches of the O'Driscolls.

The Corca Luidhe were great navigators and seamen. There are a number of reports of the battles they fought at sea and accounts of some of the tribe setting sail over the western sea and never being heard of again. It is said that St. Ciaran sailed to Rome.

The following are some records of the O'Driscolls taken from the *Annals of the Four Masters:*

1103 The son of Ua hEtersceoil, king of Corcu Laigde, went to sea with a crew of 25, and unknown is their faring or their end thereafter.

1229 Donchodd OhEtersceoil, king of Corcu Laigde died.

1472 O'Driscoll More, i.e. Fingin, the son of Mac Con, son of Mac Con, son of Fingin, son of Donagh Gud, died in his own house, after having performed the pilgrimage to St. James (Compostella in Spain), and his son Teige died penitently a month after his father's death, after having performed the same pilgrimage.

1508 O'Driscoll More, i.e. Conor the son of Fingin, son of Mac Con died. He was a valiant man in defence, the friend of the Orders (friars) and of learned men; and his son Fingin was appointed his successor after he had been liberated, for he was imprisoned in Cork for more than a year.

1585 O'Driscoll More lord of Baltimore in County Cork, namely Fingin (Florence), the son of Conor, son of Fingin, son of Conor went to the parliament held in Dublin May 1585.

In the year 352 A.D., according to the *Annals of Innisfallen* as quoted by Jeremiah J. O'Mahony in his *West Cork and its Story:*

. . . Ciaran, Bishop of Saigir, was born. In the year 402 Ciaran

51

and Declan came from Rome to preach the gospel in Ireland. Ciaran, having preached the gospel in Inis Cleire and all over Corca Luigde (Corcalee), founded a Bishop's See at Saigir in Ossory.[3]

O'Mahony also translates the following from Standish O'Grady's edition of Silva Gadelica:

Bishop Ciaran of Saigir was the first Bishop who was born in Ireland, of the west division of Leinster, called Ossory – and Laighne was his father's name (note this is not the name given him by Aengus) who was of the gentry of Ossory.[4]

St. Martin of Tours was an uncle of St. Patrick and his name was frequently used in the dedication of Patrician churches, yet there are few, if any, such dedications in the southwest of Ireland, which would seem to indicate that this area was not Christianized by Patrick. Even Professor Eoin MacNeill, a man not easily convinced, says, 'The claim by the Corca Laighe, or Darini, that they were the first to receive Christianity cannot be dismissed on the ground of improbability.'[5] D. A. Binchy points out the number of Latin loan words in use in Ireland before Palladius were almost all of a religious nature and, significantly, included no word for bishop or Irish equivalent for the Latin *episcopus*. These words were unquestionably introduced in the south and southeast of Ireland by British Christians.[6]

It may be argued that the above assumptions will not fit in with the dates given by the annalists, but the dates of the early annals were all too often at variance with each other, usually only by a year or two, but sometimes as much as ten years. Moreover, the early hagiographer tended to push the subject of his writing as far back in history as he could, to give him, her or it a respectable antiquity. In the case of St. Patrick the date of his arrival in Ireland could not have been pushed back any further, for he would then have been before Palladius!

The dating of the Patrician mission is a very controversial one upon which much research work has been done in recent years and it seems that the general corpus of learned opinion now favours 456 as the date of his arrival here on his mission and the date of his death as 493. Other complications are that Patrick's real name was Succoth and many historians claim that there were three Patricks and, indeed, Dr. Petrie claims there were seven. More evidence for a later arrival is that, in his own writings, Patrick describes the Irish as Hibernians and this word only came into use towards the end of the fifth century; before that the Irish were known as 'Scotti'. Patrick was not a Christian name as we know it today but a title of honour, as in the Roman Patrician. Incidentally, it would seem that Lady Ferguson's *The Irish Before the Conquest* is the only history in which it is mentioned that St. Patrick's two sisters, Darerca and Lupida, were captured with him by Niall of the Nine Hostages. Darerca, at least, appears in the later annals.

Ros Ailithir (or Rosscarbery) was one of the principal abbeys of the Corca Luidhe. It was a recruiting ground for the German abbey of Wurtzburg, where St. Killian of Lauragh was martyred in or about the year 687. It is recorded that 'Ross Ailithir has an appropriate rectory in the country of a certain Irishman called O Swyllyvan Barry' and Father Coombes says this is Killaconenagh, now Castletownbere: [7] The *Annals of Innisfallen* in 815 record the death of Forbasach, king of Corcu Laigde, and in 1103 they say Conchobar Ua hEtersceoil, king of Corcu Laigde, died in Ros Ailithir.

In Co. Wexford there is a very strong tradition that the area was converted to Christianity by St. Ibar, whose abbey was on the island of Beg Eire, in Wexford Harbour. There is no life of Ibar, though he is mentioned in several medieval sources, and in a passage in the life of St. Abban in the *Codex Salmanticensis* it is stated that his relicts were then still in the abbey of Beg Eire. The only connection St. Ibar would have with Beara is that he was an uncle of St. Abban, another presumably pre-Patrician saint. (Some say mother of St. Ibar but this seems unlikely.) He was a great founder of monasteries, including Killabban in the barony of Ballyadams, Leix, and Moyarney, near New Ross in Co. Wexford.

Local tradition in the barony of Forth, Co. Wexford, claims that the monastery on Our Lady's Island, which had become a place of pilgrimage by the year 600, was founded by St. Abban, nephew of St. Ibar. One of St. Abban's foundations was Fionn Magh. Father Brenan (following Archdale) in his *Ecclesiastical History of Ireland* calls the place Fionn-Magh-in-Fotharta (white field of St. Abban) and says it is 'Our Lady's Island'. O'Hanlon places it near Dublin, Shearman in Co. Carlow, Plummer and Hogan at Camross, Co. Wexford, and Colgan in Forth, Co. Wexford. In the Memorandum Rolls of Elizabeth I reference is made to 'Fynwag chapel' at Our Lady's Island, which is taken as evidence for that island being regarded as Fionn Magh. To come more up to date, in *Medieval Religious Houses: Ireland* Rev. Aubrey Gwynn S. J. and R. N. Hadcock say:

> After he had founded monasteries at Magce, St. Abban came to the region of Corcaduibhne, west Munster, and built a monastery at Cell-achaid-conchean, wherein was St. Conchenna (Acta Sanctorum - Colgan pp 615/622.) The Rev. J. M. Cronin identifies this as Killaconenagh, in the Bere peninsula on the border of Cork and Kerry, a region of several supposed foundations of St. Abban.[8]

The name Killaconenagh has been variously translated as follows:

'The wood of the rabbits' (Maziere Brady, *Records of Cork, Cloyne and Ross*), 'The church of the fasting Aiche' (Canon John Lyons, *JCHAS* vol. 3 1894), 'the church of St. Oghigjanagh' (Bishop Dive Downes, 'Visitation 1699 - 1700') and 'the church of the fair field'. Canon John Lyons says:

> 'The Church of the Fasting Aiche' = Cill Aice - n'aoinig. This verifies the pronounciation exactly. Another fact should place this rendering beyond reasonable doubt. Aengus, in the first line of his quatrain in praise of St. Aiche says: 'pious Aiche loved fastings'. She was one of the two virgin daughters of Darerca, St. Patrick's sister. Aengus says they had seventeen brothers, all bishops. [9]

Perhaps the 'the church of the fair field' above might have been Abban's Fionn Magh! Mr. Gerard Harrington gives the translation as 'the burial place of the champion of the fair' (*Southern Star*, 19.1.1979).

Chapter 6

Rossmacowen

Leaving the Bible and prehistory we carry on westward until we come to the bridge over Rossmacowen River. Here turn right towards the mountains and continue on for little more than 1 km to Park Lake. The road is sometimes wired off and cars may have to be left here, but it is only a short distance to the lake. If one turns left immediately after the lake and then right, two cliffs running parallel with the mountains will be seen. At the foot of one of these there is large oblong stone with flat sides, known locally as the 'mass rock'. Now anything known as a 'mass rock' usually turns out to be a boulder dolmen, a wedge grave or some other form of megalithic tomb, but not so in this case for all the sides of the rock are smooth, as also is the top, and there is even a narrow ridge running along the upper part of the back of the rock. In fact it looks like a genuine altar. Further along and about 9 m up on the cliff face may be found a cave known as *tig fé thalamh*, or 'the house under the ground'. It is somewhat inaccessible but it is sheltered, neat and clean, and could have made an excellent hiding place for a priest in penal days.

This area is Rossmacowen Commons and is a splendid place for walks, along the banks of the Rossmacowen River, up the Coomnagapple Glen or the steep sides of Hungry Hill.

About 800m due south of Rossmacowen Bridge, on the eastern side of the river, is a children's burial ground. Unusually for such there is an inscription on one of the headstones, which reads, 'Honora O'Sullivan Died 9 July 1815 aged 3 months'. The burial ground is rather inaccessible and it is easier to reach by going back towards Adrigole for a short distance and taking the first junction right, down to Thornhill.

West of Rossmacowen Bridge is the little village of the same name. A road runs to the bogs on the mountain top, and the first branch off this goes down to the valley of Curraduff and the Rossmacowen River; the second branch, to the left, connects with an impassable portion of the medieval road. If one takes the middle road it would be well to park the car at the first good turning place after reaching the commons lands. The road becomes rough after this, but it is good walking country.

Here are two large standing stones, and nearby a very rough circular trench in the ground. One of the stones stands on the perimeter of this circle. It may possibly be the remains of a circle of standing stones, with an outlier. In an adjoining field to the southwest is an oblong enclosure of low but broad and well-built walls and within it is a small standing stone. There is no entrance and the place is locally known as the *lios*, which means 'fort' but is a term usually used in association with fairies.

The narrow little road to Bunow leading down from Rossmacowen to the sea is unsuitable for cars. This strand is, at low tide, suitable as a bathing place for children and at high tide, for swimmers.

Near here, just over 100 years ago, lived a man named Tim Harrington, known as 'Tadhg a Varrig' because he dredged up sand from the sea bottom and sold it to the local farmers. Apparently it was not a profitable business, for he was evicted by Lord Bantry for nonpayment of rent. His only possessions were a horse and a cart, so he started business as a carrier between Castletownbere and Cork. At this he proved very successful, rapidly building up a firm reputation for his probity, financial integrity and efficiency. He opened a shop in Castletownbere, in the house next to what was formerly the Munster and Leinster Bank. He married Ellen Tobin of Schull.

A story I have had from two sources records that there were two sisters, one very pretty and the other, Ellen, rather the reverse. At the wedding the bride was heavily veiled and when she unveiled after the ceremony Tadhg discovered he was married to the ugly sister. In one version of the story he accepted the situation, merely remarking, as he looked at Ellen's limp, 'Ah well, life has its up and downs.' The other version, which I believe to be authentic, says Tadhg refused to take unto himself Ellen, and came home without her, but was persuaded by his friends and relatives that she might prove, in the long run, to be the better match and so it was. She was a good businesswoman and looked after his shops, for he had opened ones at Allihies, Eyeries and Adrigole and, possibly, Kealkil. The last reference is doubtful, but it does seem a likely place for him to open a shop.

Tadhg and Ellen had only three daughters and no sons, so they decided that these would have better opportunities for making good matches in Cork and they sold out in Beara and transferred their business to the city, where his success continued unabated. And their daughters did make good matches, one marrying a member of the Punch family, tea merchants of renown, another a Hegarty of the family well known in medical and legal circles, while the third married a Mr. Garde. In the late 1950s a Father Garde gave a retreat to the convent in Castletownbere and he proved to be a descendant of Tadhg a Varrig.

To the west of Rossmacowen, just around the bend after Waterfall post office, a lane crosses the road. A short walk up this towards the mountain brings one out onto a disused section of the medieval road, and a little to the west will be seen a 'cloghogle', or boulder burial. This is slightly unusual in that the capstone, resting on three small boulders, is a flat slab of rock instead of the usual boulder. On this there are seven shallow circular depressions, which could be the result of erosion but are probably cup-marks. A little to the west is a small standing stone and, continuing west, the medieval road emerges on to a used section of the old road.

After passing the Wheel Inn a bridge takes the road over the Owgarriff River and about 30m beyond this a path on the right side of the road leads through the little wood and up by the Owgarriff River to join the medieval road about 400m away. This is an extremely attractive walk near the river, with its ravines, many waterfalls and crystal clear pools. On reaching the medieval road one can take the unused road eastwards, or follow the road still in use to the west, or continue on up along the river. The road to the west joins up with a regular network of roads, mostly cul-de-sacs, providing a great variety of interesting walks between there and Castletownbere, a distance of not much more than 2 km.

Westward along the main road one passes the signpost to the pontoon for Bere Island, and, immediately after this, the golf course and then a grove of trees, with a lane leading seawards. This is Mill Cove, site of the residence of Lord Bantry's agent, Patrick O'Sullivan, which was razed to the ground. Patrick O'Sullivan Beare was a tyrannical landlord. One of his customs was to blow a trumpet outside the church after Mass on Sundays, summoning all the tenants to bring in his hay or turf or do whatever farming tasks he required of them.

Lord Bantry's Filane and Bere Island estates were sold in November 1853 under the Encumbered Estates Acts. Patrick O'Sullivan Beare was agent for these estates and he feared he was going to lose his mansion of Mill Cove, which was on the Filane estate, and local tradition says he went up to Lord Bantry and they re-drew the estate map to show Mill Cove outside the estate.

In my researches I came across a lease from Lord Bantry to Patrick O'Sullivan Beare for three lives, the ages of the lives being 54 years, 56 years and 59 years, on the lands of Mill Cove. The date of the lease was January 1853; and the estate was to be sold in November 1853! Lord Bantry had given Patrick O'Sullivan Beare a separate lease for Mill Cove House, so the unfortunate purchaser of the Filane estate, Lord Charles Pelham Clinton, 5th son of the 4th Duke of Newcastle, finding himself without a residence on the property, built Waterfall House. He had bought the estate free of encumbrances but hardly was the deal completed when Lord Bantry made seizures on Lord Clinton's now tenants for arrears of rent, greatly to Clinton's annoyance.

If local tradition is to be believed, Lord Bantry tried to sell the Bere Island estate to Clinton and persuaded him to inspect it although he didn't want to purchase it. However, when he found copper there he changed his mind, but, unfortunately, this copper had been borrowed from the Puxleys by Lord Bantry and planted on Bere Island! The story goes on to say that, at a function in London, Lord Clinton overheard somebody denouncing the iniquities of his Irish tenants and butted in to say the Irish tenants were not anything like as bad as the Irish landlord!

There does not seem to be any evidence for the story and no doubt it is apocryphal. There was a mine shaft drilled on the Filane property and this does not appear to have been productive, so perhaps it was there that the copper was salted.

The Clintons would appear to have been good landlords and any seizures made were for arrears due to Lord Bantry. In 1854 Lord Clinton's agent, John P. Prendergast, wrote: 'This last driving of your Lordship's so overcrowded the great circular pound at Rossmacowen that the place was a pool of gore and the bellowings of the tortured cows could be heard at the top of Hungry Hill. '[1]

In May 1905 and in July of the following year decrees were obtained and notices of eviction were served, but these would appear to have been purely nominal. A very old man, who remembered them, told me that the first house the bailiffs went to contained an old sick woman, so they did not carry out the eviction. At the second house the husband was away and only a woman and young children were there, so the eviction was not carried out there either. At the third house the furniture was all taken and left outside. The police and bailiffs sat around until dusk and then they went away, leaving the furniture behind. The tenants took the furniture back into the house and that would appear to be the end of the episode.

At Mill Cove is Cummeranassig Bridge and a few hundred metres beyond this the road has been widened at a crossroads, where there is a narrow lane leading down to the sea. Close to the sea there is, on the right side of the road, a very much ruined ring fort. Here there is a standing stone, around which are grouped, in semi-circular rows, small unmarked headstones. The place is marked on the Ordnance Survey six inch map as 'Burial ground, disused' and is probably a killeenagh, or burial place for children.

From here the road into Castletownbere is broad with little of interest, but if one crosses the main road and goes up the road towards the mountains there is much to be found. From a crossroads look northwest to see a standing stone. This one is slightly unusual in that two parallel rows of low stones seem to form a kerb leading up to it.

Back at the crossroads, turn right and come to a right-angled bend in the road. One is again on the old medieval road and if one looks through the gate facing the road here it will be obvious where the old road ran. The road up to the left passes a scattered group of houses and goes on to the bog at Derrymihan East. At one point the ground slopes sharply down to a little stream on the left with a bridge over it leading to a house on the other side of the stream. Just above here there are a couple of entrances into the right and here is the best place to leave one's car.

Go in the last lane on the right and to the left will be found a cashel, or stone ring fort. This is 22m in diameter and the walls are approximately 2m high by 1m thick. The entrance is to the south and is about 2m high. It would appear that an error was made in the building of this cashel, as the two ends of the ringwall did not quite meet. To the southeast of the cashel is a circular mound, 20m from the cashel, set into the side of the hill. It is about 6m in diameter, by about 1.60m high and on it is a standing stone, measuring .80m by .60m by .30m. About 300m to the northeast is an oblong field built of very substantial stone walls, inside which is a standing stone measuring .80m by .60m by .30m. It would seem that in this area a number of megalithic structures were incorporated into the building of modern fences, for the latter are unusually high and wide and, in one case at least, the corner of a field is bounded by a large loose-stonewall fence, distinctly curved. This is very probably the remains of a cashel.

As one continues along the medieval road towards Castletownbere, a small standing stone will be observed on the right side of the road. A little further on there is a branch road coming in from the left and in the angle between the two roads here, and giving a fine view looking down on Castletownbere, is a noteworthy group of megalithic monuments. In

Boulder burials, Derrymihan West (site 44)

the centre of the field are three fine examples of 'cloghogles', or boulder burials. The capstone of one has collapsed and the end of it is buried in the ground. On this there are circular depressions, almost certainly cup-marks. There is one built into the fence to the west; owing to its position it is difficult to examine, but the capstone is large and on one side, at least, it is supported by two smaller boulders resting upon each other, which is an unusual feature. In the adjoining field to the south is a standing stone, with a large stone slab resting on edge and running northwards from the standing stone. There is too little left of this monument to identify it exactly, but it was probably a wedge grave.

There is a strong tradition that a Norman family named Barnwall held lands in Beara about the 13th century. Rev. W. O'Halloran in *Early Irish History and Antiquities and the History of West Cork* (p. 134) says:

A man named Barnwell occupied in the 13th century the Berehaven district between Bantry and Castletown. There is little or nothing known of him and it is likely he did not sojourn here long.

Jeremiah J. O'Mahony in *West Cork and Its Story* (p. 136) states:

The Irish at this time (1461) got so powerful that the English paid to MacCarthy of Muskerry the sum of £40 per annum for protection.... The O'Sullivans drove the Barnewalls out of their territory.

Captain T. M. Keogh in *A Short Account of the History and Antiquities of Bere Island and Berehaven* (p. 14-15) refers to the O'Sullivans' migration from Tipperary to Kerry and West Cork, where they found the Carews at Dunamark, whom they drove out, and the Barnwalls at Berehaven; these were almost exterminated, with only a few escaping to Meath and Dublin.

Charles Smith in *The Ancient and Present State of the County and City of Cork* gives a version of these events and also mentions that:

The ancient nobility of this county in Henry IV's time, according to a letter then said to be wrote by the inhabitants, included the Lord Marquis Carew, whose yearly revenue was £2,200 per annum, the Lord Barnwall of Berehaven, who had £1,600 per annum....

Webb's *Compendium*, in a note on John Barnewall, Lord Trimblestown says:

His ancestors came over originally with Henry II and received large grants of land in the County Cork. On the first favourable opportunity the old proprietors, the O'Sullivans, rose and murdered the whole family save one young man, who was absent studying law in England. He ultimately returned and settled at Drimnagh near Dublin. [2]

The Abbé MacGeoghan's version is as follows:

The Barnwalls came over from Little Britany in France with William the Conqueror and to Ireland, where they became possessed of the land of the O'Sullivans, with Henry 2nd. They were dispossessed by the O'Sullivans, the Barrys, the Roches, and the de Courceys, the only representative of the family left being Lady Barnwall,who went to Dublin, where she gave birth to a son Reginald, who married a wealthy heiress, through whom he got the lands of Kilbrew and Crickstown.[3]

As Rev. Professor S. B. Barnwall points out, both Crossley's and Burke's Peerages mention that 'according to the records in the Bermingham Tower the first in Ireland was one Sir Michael de Berneval, who, 'tis said before Strongbow subdued Berehaven and Bantry.... Yet none of the standard histories of Ireland say anything about Normans as far west as Bantry before Strongbow's invasion.'[4]

Here, at last, a source is quoted, 'the records in the Bermingham Tower', but where are these records! They were returned to Ireland and burnt in the Public Record Office in 1922.

The late Mr. John Merwick of Castletownbere told me he had read somewhere that the Barnwalls at one time held Castle Dermot and this could well be. But, though the matter is being researched, we are still without evidence that the Barnwalls were definitely in Beara at any time.

There were certainly Normans here at that early date, for in a Patent dated at Oxford in 1177 King Henry II granted to Robert FitzStephen and Milo de Cogan a moiety of the kingdom of Cork, for the service of sixty knights' fees. In 1179 Robert FitzStephen and Milo de Cogan came to an agreement regarding the division of this vast estate. In 1183 Milo de Cogan, Ralph FitzStephen and Meredith FitzStephen, sons of Robert FitzStephen, were killed by a chief named Mac Tire near Lismore when they were on their way to raid Waterford. Robert FitzStephen was then besieged in Cork and was rescued by his nephew, Raymond le Gros. Robert – maddened, it is said, by the death of his two sons – died soon after and his nephew Raymond le Gros inherited his property, which inheritance was later confirmed by the king, and thus the Cork lands of FitzStephen descended to the Norman Carews.

The king at this time sent over Milo de Cogan's brother, Richard, to take over the other half of the moiety of Co. Cork. Milo had left an only child, Margaret, who married three times. Richard de Cogan would seem to have had no issue and by one of Margaret's marriages Milo's estate went to the de Courcys.

When Richard de Cogan came over to Cork he was accompanied by Robert FitzStephen's nephews, Philip and Gerald Barry, who apparently came to take over a grant of land made by their uncle, FitzStephen, to their father. These inheritances were disputed by the FitzMaurices, future earls of Desmond, on the grounds of the illegitimacy of both Robert FitzStephen and Raymond le Gros, and some writers argue that because of this the Carews could not possess the land. However, it is obvious that they did hold it, for the kings regularly called on them for their knights' fees, and they were allowed to grant wardships, marriages and sergeantships and all the other duties of a local lord. Moreover, on one occasion the king forgave Carew his knights' fees because he had been assisting him in his war in Scotland and later did likewise when Carew was fighting for him in France.

Now to bring the O'Sullivans into the picture: in 1193 the Normans drove the O'Sullivans out of Knockgraffon, on the banks of the River Suir in Co. Tipperary, near Caher, and they came down to Kerry, settling on the mainland opposite Valentia Island at a place called Ballynaflowen. Here they divided into two tribes, the clan Giolla na Flowen and the clan Giolla Mochuda. From here the clan Giolla Mochuda moved into the barony of Dunkerron and split into the MacGillacuddys and the O'Sullivans More, while the clan Giolla na Flowen moved into Glanerought and later into Beara and became the O'Sullivans Beare.

Chapter 7

Castletownbere

As one comes into Castletownbere there is a high rock on the right upon which there is a house, Castle House, site of Castle Dermot. The strip of land stretching from Bere Island through Inches to Coulagh Bay was MacCarthy property, and Castle Dermot was built about 1474 by Dermod, son of Tadg, son of Amphail, to protect these lands, which in 1594 were granted by Queen Elizabeth to Richard Beacon, author of *Solon, his Folly;* but Beacon also had lands in Bantry and Waterford and does not appear to have come near his Beara lands, though he may have sublet them. [1]

In a letter dated 31 August 1594 Richard Beacon mentions that 'his lands of Bere and Bantry purchased passed before Mr. Hugh Cuffe obtained letters.' In 1641 these lands were in the hands of the Earl of Cork but in the same year Fyneen MacDermod MacCarthy and Dermod MacFyneen MacCarthy owned Kilmacowen and possibly some of Inches, over 2,000 acres. Prior to this, in 1611, there was another grant by the king to Richard Beacon. [2] The rent was then £33.6.8 and the tenant was Valentine Browne, a ward of the king. In 1612 Ballinacallagh, Castletown, Inches and Derrykiveen each paid 9s 4d to the Earl of Desmond, which the king now granted to Owen O'Sullivan Beare.

A ploughland (modern equivalent, townland) contained 120 acres with a certain amount of rough pasturage, according to the goodness or badness of the soil. In 1738 the east ploughland of Castletownbere (Clandermot) was in the possession of Robert Trenwith, Senior, and the middle ploughland of Castletownbere was in the possession of Thomas Trenwith and his undertenants. In 1732 Thomas Trenwith (who, though a Protestant, had joined the O'Sullivans against the Puxleys) was proclaimed and a reward of £100 offered for his capture. As we have seen in Chapter 3, in 1807 one Henry Trenwith was buried in Kilcaskan and in 1811 Edward Trenwith was buried there. In 1829 Mary Ann Trenwith married Richard Sullivan.

The earliest of the name to appear so far west would seem to be Henry Trenwith who, according to the Census of Ireland 1659, was in possession of the lands of Gurteen, Bantry (126a. 1r. 17p). The name is Cornish and most of those who came to Beara from Cornwall did so on the opening of the copper mines at Allihies in 1812. The then landlords of this area were the Annesleys. The second of the name to settle in Ireland was Sir Francis Annesley, who married Dorothea, daughter of Sir John Philips of Picton Castle, Pembrokeshire, an area which, in later times, had close connections with the Puxleys of Dunboy Castle.

Brandy Hall Bridge

Dormer windows, Castletownbere

However, in April 1679 the Earl of Anglesey's daughter, Lady Philips Annesley, married Lord Mohun and in the marriage settlement some 15 manors in Cornwall were mentioned, so perhaps that was about the time when the Trenwiths arrived in West Cork.

The road from Glengarriff enters Castletownbere over a bridge whose name, Brandy Hall, is redolent of the age of non-excised wines and spirits, a trade that was carried on from the times of the Corca Luidhe, or O'Driscolls, lords of Beara as far back as the 8th or 9th century when, no doubt, as was said of them 300 years later, they were 'exhibiting to view large fleets of wine.' Offshore there are two islands, the 47-acre Dinish and the much smaller Minane.

When Sir George Carew and his army came to attack Dunboy in 1602 the Irish assumed that he would land his army on Dinish and cross from there to the mainland at Cametringane, on the western side of the bay. At one of those friendly discussions which seem to have been quite usual in those days before joining battle, the Irish pointed out the disadvantages of this course and Carew encouraged them in their assumption. He then put on a show of endeavouring to land on Dinish, but sent most of his troops around the eastern end of the island and landed them on the mainland, from where they were able to march to Dunboy behind the woods which then grew there.

Castletownbere, also known as Castletown Berehaven or Bearhaven, is an attractive town in a most impressive setting, backed by high hills and sheltered by the great mass of Bere Island in Bantry Bay, which forms a very sound and safe haven. In recent years the town has spread considerably, but there are some very charming shop fronts in the old town, and it is to be hoped that this delightful feature will not meet the usual sad fate of anything old and beautiful.

Castletownbere is not an old town. In 1810 Rev. Horatio Townsend in *A General and Statistical Survey of the County of Cork* (p. 393), ignores the place completely. All he has to say is:

The usual mode of visiting Bearhaven, even now, is by water, the voyage from Bantry, with a tolerable fair wind, being made in four or five hours. The distance by land along the old pass, which I have travelled, was thirty miles; but, expedition being impracticable from the ruggedness of the way, the time required to perform it, even for an active traveller, was from ten to twelve hours.

In 1786 Wilson, in his *Postchaise Companion*, also advises going to Castletownbere by ferry, though he is not so scathing about the landward journey. He says:

Castletownbere

The Square, Castletownbere, a century ago

From Bantry there is a ferry boat which passes to Beerhaven, being much safer and shorter than going by land around the bay. At Beerhaven the land stretches far out into the sea, forming one side of this spacious bay, and at the extremity is the island of Dursey. This is all a wild uncultivated tract, yet well inhabited.

The town only grew up with the founding of the copper mines at Allihies in 1812, and received another fillip with the development of the British naval base at Bere Island after the Napoleonic War and the First World War. [5] At the time of Townsend's visit it was merely a few fishermens' cabins around Castle Dermot.

I remember the sea washing up to the backs of the houses and the hotel on the seaward side of the town and here was a boat slip, a pier and a coastguard station. An old lady mentioned that a great-aunt had told her she saw turf being cut on what is now the square of Castletownbere. From another informant I learn that the square was once paved with flagstones from Liscannor in Co. Clare.

In 1835 Samuel Lewis found the population was 1,468. The town consisted of one long street of newly built houses, with several large shops. There were now 300 houses in the town and it was rapidly increasing in size. Belonging to the port were 4 decked boats of 20 tons burden, 12 hookers of 12 tons and 51 yawls of 4 tons which afforded employment to about 400 fishermen.

Lewis notes that a little westward of the town was the church of Kilaconenagh capable of accommodating 150 persons and built in 1812 at a cost of £461 10s 9¼ d. Divine Service was celebrated once in the church on Sundays and the principal festivals. (On 27 July 1841, during the incumbency of Rev. Thomas O'Grady, a new church on a new site in the parish of Killaconenagh was consecrated as the parish church of union of Killaconenagh, Killcatherine, and Kilnamanagh, also known as Kilmanagh, and on 24 October 1845 a house on the glebe lands of the last mentioned parish was licenced for divine service.) Lewis also refers to the large cruciform Roman Catholic church, built in the year 1822 at a cost of £1,000.

In 1835 Lewis says there were some remains of Castle Dermot and the residence of the inspector of the coast guard occupied part of its site. At this time the principal residences here were: Dunboy (J. L. Puxley), Cametringane (J. O'Sullivan), Mill Cove (P. O'Sullivan), Broderick Cottage (Major Broderick) and Seapoint (R. O'Sullivan).

At the western end of Castletownbere an avenue to the left leads to Cametringane House, now a hotel. Cametringane House and lands were leased by Thomas Hutchins from Mrs. Margaret Burke who held these lands by virtue of being the widow of Charles Annesley, who held a large share in this estate, and also in Bere Island, by virtue of being the daughter of Edward Eyre of Galway, owner of a large portion of that island. Before 1783 Mrs. Burke brought in an 'in between' landlord, Richard Mellifont. Hutchins disapproved of the system of taking in such extra landlords and he flatly refused to pay his rent to Mellifont, though he was quite willing to pay the rent to Mrs. Burke. The case went to court and dragged on some years until in 1786 the lease fell due and Mrs. Burke, who in a letter described Hutchins as 'the most obstinate man in the world', seized the opportunity not to renew it. Instead she leased the property to an O'Sullivan, very much to the indignation of Thomas Hutchins.

In 1763 James Baldwin married Mary, daughter of Daniel O'Connell, grandfather of Daniel O'Connell the Liberator. Their son Herbert Baldwin M.D. of Cork married, firstly, Miss Barbara Dunne and by her had one surviving daughter, Mary Anne Baldwin, who married John O'Sullivan of Cametringane. They had three sons, Murty O'Sullivan, born in 1835, John O'Sullivan, born in 1837 and Herbert Baldwin O'Sullivan, born in 1853. The last mentioned was later of Clohina, possibly having inherited his maternal grandfather's estate.

In 1845 John O'Sullivan of Cametringane was a magistrate for the county of Cork, and Patrick O'Sullivan of Mill Cove was, in 1856, chairman of the Berehaven Board of Guardians. In 1910 the following were amongst the magistrates for Co. Cork.

1. Major Charles W. Bowlby, Dunboy Castle, Castletownbere. He was a relative of the Puxleys and rented Dunboy Castle. He appears in *Hungry Hill* as Boles.
2. Charles Stapleton Pelham Clinton.
3. Henry J. Harrington, Cluin Hotel, The Mines, Allihies, Castletownbere.
4. Daniel D. Harrington, Castletownbere.
5. Michael Regan Harrington, Castletownbere.
6. Charles V. Handcock, Manager, Munster & Leinster Bank.
7. William Martin Murphy, Dartry, Rathmines, Dublin and the Square, Bantry.
8. Eugene O'Sullivan, B.A., Brooklyn House, Canterbury, Kent, Mill Cove, Berehaven, and Riversdale House, Coachford, Co. Cork.
9. Robert O'Brien Studdert, Dunboy Castle, Castletownbere and Kilkishen, Co. Clare. He married, as his 2nd wife, 20 March 1884, Maria Frances Puxley and no doubt rented Dunboy Castle during its vacancy. In *Hungry Hill* he appears as Robert O'Brien Spencer.

In 1700 Bishop Dive Downes, found that the 'Popish priest of

Killaghancenagh, Kilmanah, and Kilkatieran' was Teige Sullivan who had been there 20 years. [3]

In 1790 a French traveller, Charles Etienne Coquebert de Montbret, records that the priests in Beara then were Berehaven: M. Daniel Sullivan and M. Michael Sullivan, and Kenmare side: M. MacCarthy. parish of Tuassiat: M. Sullivan. [4] He goes on to remark that:

Glenerought, Bantry and the whole of Kenmare Bay is Sullivan country. A Mr. Mahoni, a catholic gentleman worth £1,000 per annum, living three miles from Nedeen, was Colonel of a company of Volunteers, all Sullivans and all well-off men enjoying from £200 to £500 a year. The Sullivans are full of personal vanity. They have their children taught English, which they speak with great purity, and they also speak latin. They dress well and affect an air of good breeding and affluence that is quite astonishing. [5]

Most of what Coquebert had to say is interesting and enlightening, but he came to Nedeen (Kenmare) via Ballyvourney and so, apparently, saw little of Beara.

Some other priests in Beara at a later period were: in 1845 Father Fitzgerald, P.P. Castletownbere; in 1859 Father Michael Enright, P.P. Castletownbere, who died 23 May 1865 aged 68 years and is buried in Rossmacowen graveyard.

In 1859 the parish priest of Eyeries was Rev. M. O'Reilly and that of Clanlaurence was his brother, Rev. John O'Reilly. They had a sister Mary, wife of Denis O'Shea, Castletownbere. She died 19 October 1871, aged 41 years, and is buried in Rossmacowen. Also buried in Rossmacowen is Rev. James Hampston, for many years a popular and zealous Catholic curate in several parishes in the diocese of Kerry, born 1800 and died 1861.

Chapter 8

Castletownbere Vicinity

Many of the archaeological sites mentioned in the Introduction are readily accessible, and there are at least half a dozen of these sites within comfortable walking distance of the town. Go out on the Kenmare road and take the first turn to the left, just by the former technical school (now a boys' primary school), and then take the next turn to the right, 100m or so up, and you will come to a short steep hill, by a bungalow. When you have passed the bungalow watch out for a gated laneway to the right. Go down this and at the end of the lane, in the first field to the north will be found a burial ground, which is site 57 on the list of Berehaven sites. It is completely overgrown and, until comparatively recently, had been quite forgotten by the local people. It would be extremely difficult to date but would certainly have been in use before St. Finian's cemetery, on the eastern side of the Castletownbere-Kenmare road, which was consecrated on 2 August 1875.

In the adjoining field to the southeast is site 47, which is marked on the Ordnance Survey map as 'Gallauns', and consists of a large standing stone, approximately 2m by 1m in size and two fallen stones of similar size. The site overlooks Castletownbere and the harbour entrance. Returning to the road, continue northward until you come to the last fence just before the two roads join and here, in the stone wall running from one road to the other, will be found site 48, a boulder burial, or dolmen. The capstone is 1.55m long by 1.94m by .50m and it rests on three smaller boulders, the steadiness of the structure being ensured by small pegstones, a feature which proves that it is not merely a glacial erratic.

A little further to the north a track curves into bogland on the left of the road (westward) and here on the Ordnance Survey six inch map is marked a 'Holy Well', which consists of a low circular mound 16.10m in diameter and approximately .50m high, on which are two holes of equal size, each measuring .80m by .40m. There is no water in these holes and the probability is that the place is a habitation site, and the holes are cooking places, though, if so, they are rather crude ones.

There is a tradition that a bishop came from the monastery on the Skelligs to convert the people here to Christianity and that he was refused permission to preach. So on his way home the bishop stopped here and cursed Beara. One of the monks with him, a better Christian, asked him would he not leave something good behind him and he agreed to make this well a place for curing diseases of animals. In those days the lords of the soil were the O'Driscolls, not the O'Sullivans who would not arrive here for another three or four hundred years, and the O'Driscolls had a perfectly good reason for refusing the bishop's request, since they were reputedly the first to teach Christianity in Ireland, as we have seen.

From here one could return to Castletownbere by the main road, a round trip of less than 3.5 km. On the Ordnance Survey six inch map there is a killeenagh marked in the field immediately north of St. Finian's cemetery, but this appears to have been completely destroyed.

The aforementioned sites are all in the townland of Foildarrig, but if one continues northwards through the Gap of Clountreem one will find some very interesting sites. Here the road branches into three, and the first site (No. 50) is in the first field between the main road and the old road higher up the hillside to the west. It is very doubtful; it may be a circular hut site but it is very much weathered and may merely be a place where hay or turf was put to dry. It is scarcely worth stopping for and it would be more advisable to take the first turn to the right, after passing through the gap. About 1.5 km down this road, after you have passed a quarry, a lane leads up to a fine standing stone about three fields in from the road, on the right (site 51), and in the adjoining field to the south is site 52, a small but very good example of a wedge grave, inside which is a stone bearing a fine set of cup-marks. A puzzling feature of these two sites is that a line of low stones curves down from the grave to the standing stone. Most people say it is merely the remains of a field fence, but a German archaeologist suggested that it was an assembly place. It might also have been a processional way.

Continue northwards along this road to the hamlet of Kilmacowen and, immediately after crossing a bridge, a road leads to the right, and about 100m along it, behind the first house on the left, is another fine standing stone (site 53). Return to the bridge and continue northwards past the former Kilmacowen school on the left and take the branch road to the right immediately after the school. After passing a quarry we come to a road leading steeply uphill to the left. From here may be seen the walls of the very interesting site of Caheravart, a hill settlement.

The site can be reached by going straight ahead until one reaches the first farm entrance on the left, turning one's car here and coming back 100m. On entering the fields here the site of a mill and its associated mill pond will be found. There is a cutting through solid rock outcrop to bring the water from the mill pond to the mill. However, the road is very narrow here and, though the hill does look rather daunting, it would be more advisable to go up it until it turns at right angles to the left. There is room to turn here. Go into the last field on the right before the top of the hill and inside the third field in will be found a standing stone, with a typical sloping top, and in the next field to the east is the great hillfort or settlement of Caheravart (site 120).

It is a large ringwall enclosure about 200m in diameter. The height of the wall is greatest on the seaward side, in this case the southern, where it reaches an imposing height of 3m, while at the northern end it falls away to a mere metre. Similarly, the width of the wall varies from 1.50m at the south to .50m at the north. There is a well running through the centre of the enclosure but this is poorly built and is obviously modern. It is interesting to compare this modern wall with the beautifully built dry walls of the ringwall.

On the northeastern side of the enclosure is a mound, 28m long by 2.50m in height, which is faced with loose stone walling. Below this mound the land is now very marshy, but it is evident that it was once drained into the mill pond. On top of the mound is a very crude stone cross, a killeenagh and a pile of stones which are almost certainly the remains of a collapsed beehive church. Behind the mound are the

foundations of two medieval rectangular houses, measuring about 11.60m by 7.30m, and the foundations of a similarly sized hut will be found below but more to the centre of the enclosure and to the east of the modern wall. Also within the enclosure have been found the sites of half a dozen or so medieval, or earlier, hut sites, at least two of which are set into the ringwall. Those that can be measured have diameters of 12.30m, 4.30m, 4.30m and 4.80m. There are at least two similar sites which are too eroded to be measured. These sites are usually overgrown in the summer months and so are difficult to find. However, the place has been taken over by the Office of Public Works as a national monument and it is to be hoped that it will be kept clear.

Stone Cross, Caheravart (Site 120)

At the foot of the adjoining hill to the south of the enclosure is the mill pond. This is now dry but it will be obvious that all the surrounding hills drained into it and one small stream running from the northeast into the pond had its sides lined with stone flags, so there would have been an ample supply of water. On the southern side of the pond will be noticed, about 2m up, a cutting through the rock and it was through this that the water flowed down to

Ogham stone, Ballycrovane (site 128)

the horizontal water mill. The lower end of the mill stream, to the southwest beneath the bushes, has been built up by stone walling on each side, and it is probable that there may have been another water mill below this. Indeed this seems to have been a country of water mills and several probable ones have been reported.

There is one certain site which may be advised of here; on the way to this ringwall settlement, where you turned to the left up the steep hill, there is an outhouse on the opposite side of the road and alongside this house runs a deep trench like a lane and after less than 100m it turns at right angles to the south. In the field at this bend are the foundations of a small house and it is clear this was another mill site.

From the ringwall enclosure of Caheravart, to the south there is a view of the two large standing stones, sites 51 and 53, and from the standing stone in the field to the left of the enclosure may be seen, on the skyline to the northwest and leaning sideways, another standing stone (site 126a) on Knockeen Hill. From this stone will be seen, to the northwest, the very fine ogham stone at Faunkil and the Woods, which bears the inscription 'Maqi son of Deccadda and grandson of Torani'. It is tempting to think that this may be a signpost and the standing stones indicators to show the way to his residence. It must be admitted, however, that the stone on Knockeen Hill is not a standing stone in the strict sense of the words, for it is nearly a large boulder resting in a crack in the rock and may be merely a glacial erratic or, more probably, a trigonometrical station. From a distance, though, it does look like a standing stone.

As regards the inscription on the ogham stone, the Decca, Deche, Deda, Daga or Dagda was an ancestral god associated with the Arxentorium tribe of the Britonic Celts, and the Roman poet Lucan, writing in the first century, mentions a Celtic god, Taranis. It is unlikely, difficult though it is to place a date on these ringwall forts, that Caheravart was in use at such an early date. There is a tradition that it was handed over to the monks when the local chief was converted to Christianity. This would have been quite usual and in Caheravart there are obvious signs of this having happened – the cross, the children's burial ground and the oblong buildings which were probably monkish – but it is impossible, in the absence of excavation, to say how long prior to this the place was in use. Consequently, the signpost/guide stones idea must be treated with caution.

In preparation of this I noted a circular enclosure about 300m northeast of Caheravart, which I had overlooked until now. Evidently there may be many more archaeological sites to be found in the area!

From Caheravart one can return to Castletownbere by the same route, or take the road to the west which leads down to join the main

Kenmare - Castletownbere road at three points. When you get down to where a junction right joins the road we are on, it is only 100m to the main road, but the junction there is a dangerous one. Consequently it would be safer, and possibly of more interest, to take the junction to the right (west) at the gate. Incidentally, the old road from Eyeries to Castletownbere ran through where this gate now is.

Continuing on the road to Eyeries, about 100m up on the left side in a field, a stone measuring 1.35m by .90m by .35m lies flat on the ground. It would seem to have been a standing stone which has fallen and broken into two pieces. Another standing stone is built into the fence on the roadside just north of this. Other bits of rock appear in the field but it is not possible to say, without excavation, whether they had been standing stones or not. Very probably it may be the remains of three standing stones, though it might have been a circle. This is in the townland of Crumpane and is site 171.

Immediately north of this, about 400m up the hillside, is site 54, still in the townland of Crumpane. It is marked on the Ordnance Survey six inch map as a 'Gallaun'. This is a very crude standing stone, showing no traces of ever having been shaped. It is 2m high by 1m wide and .50m thick, and is visible from the standing stone near the hillfort of Caheravart, and can also be seen from the main Castletownbere-Eyeries road, which runs straight toward it.

When you come out on the main road turn left back towards Castletownbere. Here the Castletownbere-Allihies road and the Castletownbere-Kenmare road form a triangle. Leaving this triangle behind, one comes to the first house on the Castletownbere road, on the right side. Immediately after this there is an entrance to a farm on the right. Park the car on the road, go down this avenue, cross a bridge over the river, continue southward for a few fields and site 55 will be found. It is not marked on the Ordnance Survey maps and consists of two small standing stones, set about 1m apart, in a fence on the bank of a small stream or drain. It is of interest in that the stream has washed away the earth from the base of the larger stone, revealing the pegstones which kept it in position. So the stream or drain came after the standing stones.

If, after crossing the bridge, you turn left along the bank of the river you will find, near a sharp bend in the river, two or three small earthen enclosures. There are three gaps in the banks of each. It is probable that they may be early furnaces for smelting iron, the holes in the banks being for bellows. The site is in the townland of Inches.

This completes the tour, which amounts to about 16 km. The roads are very narrow and call for careful driving.

Leaving Castletownbere at the eastern end of the town, turn left immediately after crossing Brandy Hall Bridge on the main road, continue past the medieval Aghista Bridge and take the next branch road to the left. Carry on along here past the rubbish dump, through a small wood, and after 1.6 km the road widens and commons land commences. Park the car here and walk up the road for 100m or so and, near the first bend, down to the right in marshy ground, will be seen a very good example of a ruined circular hut site. It is built in the corbelled style, the diameter of the interior is 4.80m and the walls are approximately 2m high. A remarkable feature of the hut is that, though it is below the level of the surrounding marshy ground, it is very dry inside. These huts were built by placing flat stones on top of and overhanging each other until the gap became small enough to be covered by a single flagstone, or they were quite frequently roofed with a thatched roof. The latter had the advantage of allowing smoke from a fire to escape more easily. They are often called 'beehive huts' and are still in use in many parts of the world. I have been told of a wedge grave further up this road but I have not yet had an opportunity to inspect it.

A pleasant short walk of less than 3 km is to turn left up the Tallon road, at the western end of Castletownbere. In a field to the west of the road, shortly after passing the first bend, will be found a small killeenagh (site 58). A little further on, past the cemetery and around the next bend, as one comes within sight of the harbour entrance, a small well-shaped standing stone is built into the fence between Droum North and Droum South (site 64), and in the next field to the northwest is a very similar stone. In the fourth field on the right of the road after the bend where it turns away from the sea a fallen standing stone lies on the ground. It measures about 2m long by 1m wide. This is site 62 and is in Droum South. With the exception of the killeenagh, none of these appear on the Ordnance Survey map. Shortly after this one comes out on the main Castletownbere-Allihies road and can turn right for the town or, if one wishes to extend the walk a little, continue across the road down to the ruins of Killaconenagh Church (site 65), which is on the northern side of the Creevoge River, in the townland of Curradonohoe.

From the Monastic Map of Ireland this site would appear to have been a nunnery rather than a monastery. In the Decretal Letter of Pope Innocent III (1198 - 1216) the parishes west of Kilmocomogue (Bantry) are given as Cellechdach (Killeacac or Killough), Cellmana, (Kilmanagh or Allihies), Cellchattigern (Kilcatherine) and Cellmoceogain (Kilmackowen). It will be noted that Killaconenagh does not appear therein. It does, however, appear in a Taxation Roll of Pope Nicholas in 1291 when Dermicius Shehan was vicar of Killaconenagh and prior of Rosscarbery.

In 1615 Thadeus M'Donnell O'Sullivan was rector of Kilmanowe and Kilcatherine, and vicar of Killaconenagh, Kilcaskan, Kilcroghan and Durrus. He would appear to have conformed, for he was instructed to enforce the ordinances for the Reformation in Beara and Bantry. It is unlikely that he troubled himself much with this, if he ever came here at all.

In 1634 Killaconenagh is recorded as being attached to the priory of Ross, the vicar was Thaddeus O' Sullivan and the impropriate tithes were the property of the Earl of Castlehaven.

The Tuchets, Lords Audley of Heleigh Castle in Staffordshire and Earls of Castlehaven in Cork, had settled in Ireland in 1616. They were, strangely enough, Catholics and when Bishop Dive Downes made his visitation here in 1699 and 1700 he found the church unroofed, its timbers having been taken by Sir George Carew for the siege of Dunboy in 1602, and the Countess of Castlehaven had the rectory, worth about £18 per annum, and the bulk of the tithes. She also had half the tithes of Cape Clear.

In 1777, on the death of John Talbot, 8th Earl of Castlehaven, without issue, the earldom of Castlehaven became extinct, but the barony of Audley descended to George Thicknesse, eldest son of his sister Elizabeth, and he became the 21st Baron Audley. He took the additional name of Tuchet and the arms of Tuchet and Audley. On 21 July 1828 his son, George John Thicknesse Tuchet, Lord Audley, Baron Audley of Heleigh Castle and Count of the Holy Roman Empire, mortgaged the impropriate tithes of 74 plowlands, 3 gneeves of the parish of Killaconenagh to Jarman Hope, butcher, of Epsom, Surrey, for a loan of £1,000. On 8 August 1829 he sold these tithes and his lands in Berehaven and Carbery to Daniel Edward Stephens of Commercial Road, Middlesex, England. In 1837 these tithes were impropriate to Ludlow Tonson, Lord Riversdale, Lord Bishop of Killaloe, Kilfenora, Clonfert and Kilmacduagh, of Clarisford House, Killaloe, Co. Clare, the bishop who ordained our long-lived cleric, Dean Halahan, of whom we shall hear more later.

The graveyard of Killaconenagh is a sad affair; there are some very interesting tombstones but the place is very overgrown. It has been cleaned up a few times in recent years but the overgrowth keeps catching up and no authority will accept responsibility for the place. In 1975 a group of children cleaned it up and recorded 49 memorial inscriptions, a remarkable job in the circumstances. One inscription is to Helena Anketell. Most of the inscription is unreadable but the last few lines read: 'May she in heaven take eternal rest, The age of Christ when she left her friends Seventeen hundred 27 years.'

The Anketell family do not appear to have had any connection with this area, or only a very slight one. John Anketell, born at Newmarket,

Aghista Bridge, a century ago

Stone circle, Derreenataggart (site 66)

Co. Cork and died there in 1638, married Lucy, daughter of Mervin, 2nd Earl of Castlehaven, and Mervin's son James, the third earl, had, in 1634, the tithes of Killaconenagh. Sylvester O'Sullivan of Derreen, Lauragh, second son of Morty O'Sullivan, agent for Lord Lansdowne, succeeded his father in 1776; earlier he had married a Miss Anketell. She is said to have been a very haughty person and Lord Lansdowne, in his book *Glanerought and the Petty Fitzmaurices*, suggested that she was one of the family of that name who lived in Newmarket.

Other names that appear on memorial slabs in this graveyard are: Batt, Birmingham, Bowdler, Baker, Bunchill, Carthy, Crowley, Caulfield, Dwyer, Fitzgerald, Greenways, Guthrie, Harrington, Harper, Higginbotham, Hodnett, Jeffers, Kingston, Kelly, Longmore, Leal, Martin, Masterman, Mealy and Power. The full list of these inscriptions is in the Cork County Library, Castletownbere, entitled F.L.Y. Project No. 158 - 1975. 'Heritage of the Graveyard', by Ide O'Neill and others.

What has been described as the ideal short tour for archaeological tourists, a round of about 12.5 km, may be found by taking the road to the right, opposite the children's playground, at the western end of Castletownbere. Just past the next corner will be seen, on the northern side of the road, a stone standing in a field. This is site 59 Derreenataggart Middle. On the other side of the road there is another standing stone and in the adjoining field to the north will be seen a much more crudely shaped stone: these two stones comprise site 60. About half a dozen fields to the west there is another standing stone (site 61) and it is in use as a gate post. It came to light through the observation of a 13-year-old boy who noticed that one of two gate posts could be moved by hand, but the other was firmly set in the ground and could not be budged. This site is more readily accessible from the main road. Pass the new bungalows west of Castletownbere, then an old house on the right and west of this before one gets to the next batch of bungalows a gated lane goes to the right and this will lead to site 61.

But to continue our tour: from site 59 keep on across the bridge over the Creevoge River and take the first turn to the left and a short distance up this road, 3 km from Castletownbere, and in the townland of Derreenataggart, will be found site 66. This is on the right of the road and is a splendidly situated circle of standing stones. There are 10 stones in the circle, two of which have fallen and, as is usual, the highest and lowest stones are opposite each other. There is a groove and some possible cup-marks on one of the fallen stones and this stone may, possibly, have rested on two of the others. There is a low, furze-covered mound to the west of the circle and the former owners had a family tradition that this should not be ploughed as there was a layer of burnt stones beneath. Circles of standing stones have, on excavation, produced cremated burials and it would seem that these may have been of a ritualistic nature, so this mound was probably the place where the cremation took place here.

Fulachta fiadh or, as they are sometimes called, 'deer roasts', are cooking sites. They are found in great numbers in Ireland but scarcely anywhere else. They consist of a horseshoe-shaped mound of burnt stones and charcoal in or near a marshy place or stream. In the hollow of the mound there is a hearth which is usually built of flat stones. Outside this hearth and between it and the stream or marshy place is a trough, usually made of well-shaped wooden planks. There were two methods of cooking, boiling or roasting. To boil, a fire was lit in the hearth and when the stones were red-hot the water was let in and when it boiled, the joint, tightly covered with rushes, was put in the hearth until it was cooked. To roast, a fire was lit in the hearth, and, possibly, another on the bank rising from the hearth, in which latter fire small stones would have been heated. When all were red-hot, the debris of the fire was scraped out, the rush-covered roast placed in the hearth, and the hot stones from the fire on the bank were pushed in on top of the roast.

These cooking sites were usually found in the nearest wet place to a stone circle and such is the case here, there being one in the marshy field adjoining the field containing the circle of standing stones. There is a good gap so it is easy to get into the field, which is to the east, but it is marshy. Site 67 consists of the usual circular mound, the stone-lined hearth and many loose stones. The hearth is lined with stone slabs and measures about 1m long by .50m wide and .50m deep.

Continuing 1.5 km westward along this road one comes to site 73, in Teernahillane. This is on the right or northern side of the road, in marshy ground, and consists of a shallow circular mound, about 30m in diameter, 1.50m high at the edge and about 2m high in the centre. There are faint traces of a fosse or trench around it. It is obviously a habitation site, a platform fort or, though unlikely, it might even be a moated grange, which would be very exciting in view of the scanty evidence for Norman settlement here. However, the moated grange is a type of antiquity with which I am unfamiliar and, in any case, it would require excavation to decide the matter. Moated granges were introduced by Normans when they had settled in captured lands and they were more residential in character than the warlike mote and bailey. They became highly developed and many exist in England today, some still in residential occupation.

Site 74 is on the opposite side of the road here, a little to the east, and it is another platform fort but has been badly damaged by quarrying.

About 400m further west, on the left side of the road, is site 75. This is a boulder dolmen or boulder burial, not marked on the Ordnance

Survey maps. It consists of a boulder measuring 1.40m by 1.50m by .10m, resting on three smaller boulders. A cup-marked slab of stone lay resting against this boulder, but the slab is now broken into three pieces. Standing by the boulder burial are two standing stones, one measuring 1.40m by .80m by 80m and the other 1m by .70m by .27m. These two stones have been articially shaped.

From this site, on the skyline to the northwest, will be seen another megalith, in the townland of Coulaghard. This is a good example of a wedge grave with an unusual feature, an outlying standing stone about 20m from the grave. The site is more accessible from the northern side of the peninsula, from the townland of Coulagh.

Another 3.5 km brings us to the junction with the road over Knockoura, the old road to Allihies. There are magnificent views from here and it is excellent walking country, but the road is very rough and unsuited to cars. Of this road over Knockoura Lady Chatterton in 1838 says, 'The ascent of Knockoura mountain is very steep – even a light jaunting car can with difficulty be drawn up.'[1]

Turning left at this junction will bring us to the main road a few hundred metres away. Immediately after turning left there is, close to the road on the lefthand side, a small group of low standing stones. They have obviously been placed there, but for what purpose is quite indeterminate.

Immediately on reaching the main road, on the left and in the second field in from the road will be found a most unusual site, No. 72 Clonglaskan. It is marked on the Ordnance Survey six inch map as 'Gallauns'. It was for many years completely overgrown and in or about 1920 a visiting archaeologist described it as 'one, or at the most two standing stones' and it was only when the place was cleared of scrub and gorse by voluntary labour in 1969 that the full extent of the site could be seen. There was a semi-circle of six very large standing stones, the arc showing that it was not possible for it ever to have been a circle. Within the arc is a boulder dolmen, around which is a small circle of five or six low standing stones. Two of the large standing stones have fallen. One fell onto the boulder dolmen and in doing so forced out one of the boulders. To the northeast of the boulder dolmen lies a similarly sized boulder on the ground, unsupported. An earthen bank slopes up towards the boulder dolmen. This may have been used to roll up the boulder to get it into position. The whole is enclosed by a shallow trench; hence it is entitled to the term 'henge monument'.

Heading back towards Castletownbere across the bridge over the Inchinagat River, pass the old unused Cahergarriff school and take the next turn to the left. Park at the farm 400m or so up. Immediately behind the farm will be found another interesting site, No. 69 Fanahy. It is marked on the Ordnance Survey map as 'Gallauns'. There is one large standing stone in position and two more lie on the ground, one of which fell in 1969. The other has cup-marks on it which would indicate a burial, so it may never have been standing. There are more cup-marks on what appears to be rock outcrop, but may be a partially covered rock, possibly over a grave. The owner of the land told me that there were a lot of stones in this field but they had been removed to clear the field, and were used to build fences. The possibility is that the place may have been prehistoric burial ground.

Sites 70 and 71, both in Fanahy, are not marked on the Ordnance Survey map. They are about 400m due north of site 69. Follow the lane northwards until it veers away to the right, then take to the marshy field on the left and at the northern end of this field will be found a circular hut site (No. 70). This is about 6m in diameter, the present height of the wall is about .50m and the entrance is to the south. The wall is built of stone and earth.

Site 71 is in the adjoining field to the northwest. The site is a puzzling one. Five small standing stones form a slight curve and another well-shaped standing stone stands about 30m away. At first sight it suggests the remains of a circle with an outlier, but the arc formed by the standing stones is such that it does not seem it could ever have formed a circle.

About 700m back towards Castletownbere a turn to the right leads down to the gate into Dunboy estate, and one to the left up to a group of houses at Oakmount, said to have been a Cornish miners' settlement but more likely to have been one for the workers on the Dunboy estate. Here lived Edward Puxley, an illegitimate son of one of the Puxleys of Dunboy. He acted as estate manager of Dunboy and died in 1840 aged 84. He was Ned Brodrick in the novel *Hungry Hill*.

When Thomas Johnson Westropp was making a survey of the promontory forts of Beara and Bantry in 1921 he was told of a stone with five bullauns called fairy basins near here, which he could not find. I am not surprised for I have always had difficulty in finding them! Enter a gateway on the right at the upper side of a row of outhouses, and bear to the left. Follow the track across a marshy field, keeping more to the right or eastern side of the field. A layer of rock outcrop, in several sections, runs along the northern end of this field and the bullauns are on top of the first section. Bullauns were used for grinding grain, usually found near a monastery. The fact that here there are five might imply, as would the term 'fairy basins', that they were used for ritualistic purposes, such as the worship of grain and corn. Certainly, they are too close together to permit of five people working side by side!

Iron is said to have been smelted here, but I have not been able to

82

trace any smelting sites and so far I have found only one written reference to iron smelting near Dunboy. There is a place called Eskenacarten (the little place of the forge) near Oakmount, and when the Creevoge River was being cleared out some years ago iron pyrites were found.

Bullauns, Oakmount (site 68)

Chapter 9
West of Castletownbere

The last old house at the western end of Castletownbere, on the northern side of the Allihies road, is the former Lancet Lodge (now Ivy Lodge), which was the residence of the Armstrongs, doctors who ministered to the sick for many years here. Philip Andrew Armstrong, M.D., J.P., died 10 May 1892 aged 92. His wife, Charlotte Louisa, died 23 July 1904 aged 80. Their son James Balin Armstrong died 10 January 1906 aged 52. George William Frederick Armstrong, M.D., R.N., died 28 January 1893. His wife, Ellen, died in Cork 10 October 1941 aged 84. Fanny Rosa Louisa Armstrong died 7 March 1881 aged 22, Charlotte Louise Armstrong died 22 November 1886 aged 19 and Elizabeth Catherine Armstrong died June 1887.

In 1859 the medical officer of the Dispensary District of Castletownbere was P.A. Armstrong, L.R.C.S.E., and that of Kilcatherine, M.B. Lefebure, M.R.C.S.L. In 1910 the medical officer for the Dispensary District of Castletownbere was Dr. J. H. Lyne and for the Dispensary District of Kilcatherine Charles Harrison, L.R.C.P. Edin., L.F.P.S. Glasg.

The Castletown (Berehaven) Union Board of Guardians met on Thursdays; the chairman was Henry Harrington of Cluin, Allihies, and the vice-chairman Thomas F. McCarthy of Castletownbere. The clerk of the Union, Rural District Council and superintendent registrar was Michael J. Donovan. The medical officer was Dr. M. J. Hayes. The Rural District Council met on alternate Thursdays, the chairman being Maurice D. Power of Drumlave, Adrigole, and the vice-chairman M. T. Hanley, Castletownbere.

One day in the year 1835 a labourer came across the mountains to get Dr. Armstrong to come and see his wife, who was ill, and on the way, by the side of a mountain track, he found a tiny shoe. He brought it with him and gave it to Dr. Armstrong, who gave it to his sister who passed it on to her niece, and from her it passed to the niece's cousin, Lady Coghill of Castletownshend. One of her sisters was Dr. Edith Somerville who, in joint authorship with her cousin Violet Martin (who wrote under the pen name of Martin Ross), published many tales of Irish life and was a talented painter. When Dr. Somerville went on a lecture tour in America she took the shoe with her and it was examined at Harvard University under microscope. The shoe was about 2 7/8 inches (73 mm) long and was made, apparently, from mouse skin. It was stitched with very fine hand-stitches and had tiny eyelets, but without laces, and was about 7/8 of an inch (22 mm) in width. It was similar in style to shoes of the 18th century, but it was too narrow to be a doll's shoe. Where it came from, by whom it was made and why, and how it came to be on a remote mountain is all a mystery. The most remarkable thing about the shoe is that it shows sign of wear. Edith Somerville, in *Irish Memories* (London: Longman's, Green & Co., 1917) gives a description of it which differs slightly from my memory of the descriptions given me years ago.

West along the Allihies road from Castletownbere, just opposite the playing field, a road branches to the right which goes down to Glebe House and Killaconenagh graveyard. We have already had a look at Killaconenagh, but there is one item of interest we have overlooked.

About the middle of the last century it was noticed that the graves of recently interred corpses were disturbed and, on investigation, it was found the corpses were missing and the tradition grew up that an enchanted eel, or piast, came down from a lake on Knockoura and robbed the graves, probably adapted from or confused with the Lough Deade legend on Hungry Hill. 'Locha Deadha were on Hungry Hill and Locha modoolig there, in Coom a doolig, had a piast or enchanted eel; he issues from its waters when it freezes and is heard roaring fearfully but does no harm.' However, many accepted the 'monster' legend, though some suggested it might be an alligator or crocodile.

One of my most reliable informants told me his mother told him that two of her sisters died within a year and were buried in Killaconenagh. When they were burying the second they took up the coffin of the first and found the lid was broken and the body gone. The grave was not noticeably disturbed and the family felt that it was unlikely that a monster would fill in a grave after robbing it. Moreover, the damage to the coffin lid did not look as if it were caused by an animal. Consequently, they decided that the story about the monster robbing the graves was put out by the body snatchers to account for the missing corpses. Eventually, the monster, or the story, was killed and an inscription on his tombstone testifies to the battle Captain Mark O'Sullivan had in his destruction of it.

Captain Mark was an officer in the British army, a son of John O'Sullivan of Coulagh, brother of Captain Patrick O'Sullivan, who died in 1832, and of Margaret O'Sullivan who married John O'Sullivan of Inches, and had a son, Morty of Inches. In a public house one night in 1815 Captain Mark picked a quarrel with his nephew, Morty, and killed him in a duel. Tradition says that this was to enable him to get his hands on the Inches lands and that, moreover, in fighting the duel Captain Mark cheated. Another of Captain Mark's brothers was John O'Sullivan of Coulagh, who married Maria, daughter of John Segerson, and had a son, Morty O'Sullivan, who was the father of John O'Sullivan, of Cametringane.

Morty O'Sullivan of Inches, killed by Captain Mark, had three sisters: Hanora, who married Alexander O'Driscoll of Crookhaven, Ellen, who died without issue and Mary, who married Bennet of Schull.

A story on a somewhat similar theme was told to me by another good informant, the late Tim O'Sullivan of Droum (Tim the Master). His grandfather was a teacher in Kilmakilloge School and his salary was £10 per annum. Lord Lansdowne gave all the teachers a dinner in the Lansdowne Arms Hotel in Kenmare and doubled their salaries. In those days there was no bridge across the Sound on the Glengarriff road and when Mr. O'Sullivan arrived there he found the ferryman had gone home, so he took off his clothes, tied them on his head and swam across. Dressing himself again he continued on his way and overtook four men carrying a coffin. One of the men beckoned him to help carry the coffin and he did so, but, mindful of the old legend that if you meet men carrying a coffin at night they are fairies and if you speak to them you will be in their power, he kept his mouth shut.

Near Kilmakilloge the men turned up towards the mountain and Mr. O'Sullivan continued on his way. Realizing with what scepticism such a tale would be received, he never mentioned the incident until years later, when at a wake the subject of ghosts and fairies cropped up and he told this tale. An old man looked at him and said, 'Did you not know who was there? Did you not know it was myself and my three sons? My daughter died in Kenmare and was buried there. We went over at night, dug up her coffin, brought it back here and buried it behind the house until such a time as her body would be no use to the body snatchers. We then took it back and replaced it in the grave at Kenmare.'

At that period there was a school of anatomy in Cork, which created a demand for bodies, and in some of the cemeteries in and around Cork there are watch towers and mortsafes to protect the newly interred from the body snatchers. Mortsafes were iron cages into which a coffin could be locked until the remains were decomposed. There is also a watch tower in Tisaxon, Kinsale and another in Kinsale Abbey.

The Protestant glebe house is adjacent to Killaconenagh graveyard. On 20 June 1818 Rev. Cox Harris was admitted vicar of Killaconenagh and on 11 May 1819 he applied for permission to build a new glebe house at Killaconenagh, 'the present building being a miserable thatched cabin, and nearly a ruin.' The new glebe house was built in 1820 at a cost of £867 13s 10½ d.

Rev. Cox Harris died on 9 June 1839 and was succeeded by Rev. Thomas O'Grady on 21 August 1839, who ministered here until he transferred to Kilcoleman, diocese of Cloyne, in 1852.

O'Grady came from a very ancient and talented Co. Limerick family who claimed Milesian descent and had strong Celtic affiliations. Dr. O'Brien, Bishop of Cloyne, in his *Irish and English Dictionary* (p. 514) assigns Conal Eachluath, King of Munster 366 A.D. and sixth in descent from Oilliol Olum (of the race of Heber, eldest son of Milesius), as the common ancestor of the O'Gradys and O'Briens. The O'Briens having gained the ascendant, the O'Gradys acknowledged the paramount sway of Brian Boroimhe and became subchiefs under him.

Rev. Thomas O'Grady in 1830 was curate of Killeady, Co. Limerick, and in 1831 he was curate of Kilmoe, Co. Cork. On 21 January 1837 he married Susannah, daughter of Joshua Doe, **Carrigmanus, Co.** Cork; their sons were William Waller O'Grady, rector of Bantry, Standish James O'Grady (born 1846), and Carew O'Grady of Carrigmanus House, Co. Cork, who married Florence, daughter of James Hingston of Aglish and had three sons and a daughter. Rev. Thomas also had two daughters, Mary and Esther Julia.

His mother wanted the second son, Standish, to become a clergyman and he did try it, but his nature was too broad and too unconventional for a Church of Ireland clergyman, so he achieved the Bar instead, but he was not a great success and never made much money, though he did have a small but steady income as a leader writer for the *Daily Express*. His first schooling was at the local parish school in Castletownbere, until he was 10 years old when he went to the Tipperary Grammar School, then under the headmastership of Dr. Ryder, noted for his spartan upbringing of the boys in his charge. He then went on to Trinity College in Dublin and his great interest in life became the fostering of the Celtic Revival. At a meeting in connection with this attended by many of the elite of Dublin society, including the Lord Chief Justice of Ireland, O'Grady, who was rather drunk, as indeed were most of the company, said, 'We are here tonight to found a Celtic Cultural Society; that's not important! Then we will found a Celtic Literary Society; that's not important, but after that we will found a Celtic Revolutionary Society and *that* will be important!' And everybody, including the Lord Chief Justice, cheered lustily.

O'Grady only entered politics twice, first when he published a pamphlet entitled *Toryism and the Tory Democracy*, in which he pointed out to the landlords, with a scathing invective worthy of Swift, that their class was doomed. The second occasion was on publication of the Childers Commission, which showed that since the Act of Union Ireland was being overtaxed to the extent of £250,000,000. He threw himself into the subsequent agitation with all his powers in the hope of uniting the nation in one common policy.

It was sad that so few of the right people recognized the quality of his novels. He could get no Irish publisher to publish them and had to do so at his own expense. In about 1898 O'Grady realized that journalism in Dublin was an unprofitable business, so he took on the editorship of the *Kilkenny Moderator,* during which he co-operated with the Hon. Otway Cuffe and his sister-in-law, Lady Desert, in their efforts to provide employment, an object very dear to his heart. Their interests were wide, and I have seen a photograph of an amateur drama group in which appeared Lady Desert, Standish O'Grady and the late Dr. E. M. Fahy's father, who was then a typesetter in Kilkenny.

Maria la Touche, wife of John la Touche of Harristown, Co. Kildare, was a daughter of the Countess of Desert by her second husband and she was excessively fond of introducing the fact into conversation. However, she could not stand her noble mother's friend, Standish O'Grady, and always referred to him scornfully as 'that man'!

At the end of three years O'Grady gave up editorship of the *Kilkenny Moderator* in order to devote his attention to his own paper, the *All Ireland Review,* most of whose articles were written by himself, but he gave preference to printing articles that otherwise would never have got published. It had a very varied list of subscribers, including Lord Ashbourne, Lord Dufferin and Lord Castlemaine, as well as John O'Leary, Maude Gonne and Arthur Griffith. William O'Brien said that it was the only paper in the three kingdoms that did not irritate him.

By 1908 the sale of O'Grady's books had increased, his family were now out in the world and he had been awarded a Civil List pension, so he closed down the *All Ireland Review* and retired. His doctors had advised that he seek a warmer climate and he went to the north of France, then to the south of England, and thence to the Isle of Wight where he died in 1926. By the end of his life he had published some 27 books. (See Appendix B.)

He had married Margaret Allen, daughter of Rev. William Allen Fisher of Kilmoe, where his father had been curate. They had three sons, Carew, Hugh and Con.

Rev. Thomas O'Grady was succeeded as incumbent of Killaconenagh Union on 25 November 1862 by Rev. John Halahan, the long-lived clergyman we have mentioned before. He was a friend of Henry Lavallin Puxley, and took the services at Adrigole Church, which the Puxleys attended, apparently because they did not like Rev. Thomas O'Grady. The services at Ardgroom were taken by the other curate, Rev. James Goodman, another cleric of note.

Rev. John Halahan was born in Dublin 23 October 1823, only child of Captain Thomas Halahan, R. N., by his wife Catherine, only child of Peter Dufour, and grandson of John Halahan, first Professor of Anatomy at the College of Surgeons, Dublin. Educated at Trinity College Dublin, he was ordained deacon 6 December 1846 and priest in 1848, both at

Killaloe by Bishop Ludlow Tonson (Lord Riversdale) on Letters Dismissive of Bishop Kyle of Cork. It is not clear why Halahan was ordained by Lord Riversdale, but the latter did own a lot of land in Beara. He would also appear to have been a descendant of Richard Tonson, collector of revenue for the port and district of Baltimore, who, as we shall see, had a narrow escape from the Puxleys and the O'Sullivans in September 1732.

Halahan was curate of Killaconenagh Union from 1846 to 1862, when he succeeded Rev. Thomas O'Grady. He was appointed Precentor of Ross in 1884 and Rural Dean in November 1865. He resigned 11 March 1918, died in Bantry 8 September 1920 and was buried in Castletownbere.

In November 1865 Rev. Halahan married Harriet, only daughter of Rev. Strong Sargent and had five sons and one daughter, Jane Eliza, whose first husband was Henry Edmund Lavallin Puxley. Dean Halahan and his wife Harriet are said to be the originals of Rev. Tom Callaghan and Aunt Harriet in the novel *Hungry Hill*, and their daughter Jane Eliza the original of Jinny Callaghan.

Rev. James Goodman was born 22 September 1828, son of Rev. Thomas Chute Goodman, rector of Dunurlin, diocese of Ardfert, and grandson of Rev. John Goodman, rector of Kemerton in Gloucestershire. James Goodman had a successful career in Trinity College Dublin, obtaining a Hebrew prize and Irish scholarship in 1847, besides several premiums for proficiency in the Irish language. He was a member of the Senate and Professor of Irish in 1879. In 1852 he was curate of Creagh in the diocese of Ross and in 1858 he was appointed curate of Killaconenagh, residing at Ardgroom, where he remained until 1867, when he became vicar of Abbeystrewry.

Rev. Goodman was reared at Baile Aimin, west of Dingle, then wholly Irish-speaking. Before he went to school he was an accomplished player on the flute and later became an expert player of the Irish bagpipes. At the age of 24 he was on the council of the Ossianic Society. While serving at Ardgroom he noted down his collection of Irish traditional music, a great number of the original notations being made from the playing of Thomas Kennedy, an old piper who had followed him from Dingle to Ardgroom. His collection, contained in four volumes now in the library of Trinity College Dublin, comprises over 2,300 pieces, many of these derived from printed sources or from the manuscripts of fellow collectors. His net contribution to the store of notated music would be around 900 airs, a figure that puts him among our foremost collectors. He published various tracts in Irish and a hymnbook in that language. He was a member of the Royal Irish Academy and the Royal Society of Antiquaries of Ireland.

In October 1852 Rev. Goodman married Charlotte, sister of Rev. Robert King, author of the *Church History of Ireland,* and produced three sons: Francis George, Godfrey, M.D., and James, M.D. He died on 18 January 1896.

About 3 km west of Castletownbere a branch road to the left leads to the entrance to the mansion and castle of Dunboy. This road continues on to the right and behind the castle. Just around the bend a road branches to the right and continues to the very pleasant natural harbour of Pulleen with a stream flowing into it under an ancient bridge and over a salmon leap. The stream comes down from a lake just a little to the north. On the opposite side of the cove there is a cave, where seals may be often seen. Above the cave there is a large circular funnel-like hole in the ground, the bottom of which is blocked up with large stones.

Standish O'Grady chose this area as the locale of his novel *The Chain of God,* in which two boys get washed up into a cave high up on the cliff face, where one of them sees the ghost of a monk and later finds his manuscript biography and his store of ring money from which they made the Chain of Gold to effect their escape. The gist of the story hinges on the discovery of a place named Rohar and the third chapter in the book is entitled 'Rohar discovered': it was this chapter that discovered for me Standish O'Grady and Castletownbere.

One day, in a secondhand book shop, I picked up the book, opened it at Chapter 3 and read 'Rohar is the local designation of a promontory on the west coast of Ireland. It runs westwards from the little posting town of Ahascragh.' I knew Ahascragh and one couldn't talk of a 'peninsula' running from it, as it is far inland in Co. Galway. So, in curiosity I bought the book and it was not long before I realized that for 'Ahascragh' I should read 'Castletownbere' and that the Reverend Thomas Freeman in the novel was the Reverend Thomas O'Grady, rector of Berehaven, whose estate at Three Castle Head is mentioned in the novel. There would appear to have been a place called Rohar on Bere Island, one of the tenants in 1853 being Timothy MacCarthy Rohare of Derrycreeveen. The Piper's Rocks at the harbour entrance are also mentioned, together with Maulin, Lough Katherine, Pulleen and Cnoc-an-Dree. Similarly, O'Grady's novel *Lost on du Corrig* is based on his own family.

If, instead of turning down to Pulleen, one continues straight up the hill behind Dunboy, one comes to Disert, from where there is a fine view of Bantry Bay, Berehaven and the Slieve Miskish and Caha mountains. It is also a good place to start cliff walks with good coastal views, including the harbour entrance and the Piper's Rocks, right around to Pulleen. Both these roads are cul-de-sacs but there is ample turning room at the end of each.

Chapter 10

The Puxleys and the O'Sullivans

A visit to the grounds of Dunboy should not be missed, especially when the rhododendrons are in bloom. The burnt-out mansion of the Puxley family was built in three different stages, by far the oldest being the tower house at the western end, but it is very difficult to date this. It may have been built by the O'Sullivans about the middle of the 14th century but, if so, the windows were undoubtedly enlarged at a later date. It was certainly here that the Puxleys resided when they first came to Berehaven, by which time the O'Sullivans were in Dursey, Coulagh, Inches and Rossmacowen. According to *Burke's Landed Gentry* vol. 3 1970:

> Henry Puxley, of Ahascragh, Co. Galway, born 1685 married and had, with other issue,
> (1) Henry, married a daughter of Captain Richard Goodwin, and aunt of Rev. Thomas Goodwin, Rector of Berehaven, Co. Cork.
> (2) John Puxley, of whom presently.
> (1) Eleanor Puxley married — Burke and had issue.
> (2) Mary Puxley married Patrick FitzSimon of Liscure, Co. Galway and had issue.
> These names, Burke and FitzSimon re-occur later in the Puxley history.
> The younger son, John Puxley, of Dunboy Castle, Castletown Berehaven, Co. Cork, J. P., obtained a grant of lands around Dunboy and the new Dunboy Castle 1723, for services rendered to the English army, born 1710, married Mary, daughter of James Hayes, of Kinsale and was murdered by Morty Oge O'Sullivan, Chief of the O'Sullivans, 10th March 1754.

The 1886 edition differs slightly from the above.

> John Puxley J. P. Galway, settled about 1730 at Dunboy, Co. Cork, with Henry, his brother, who married a daughter of Captain Richard Goodwin and aunt of the Rev. Thomas Goodwin, Rector of Berehaven. John married Mary daughter of James Hayes Esq. of Kinsale.

There is no mention here of the grant of lands. Local tradition and A. J. Fetherstonehaugh in 'The True Story of the Two Chiefs of Dunboy' says: 'Henry Puxley appears to have been agent to Mr. Eyre, one of the landlords of Berehaven.'¹ This seems highly probable.

Robert Annesley, a friend of King James I, left England in 1606 and settled in Ireland, on the plea that it would be easier to practise the Catholic religion here. He was succeeded by his eldest son, Sir Francis Annesley (mentioned in Chapter 7), who for 40 years filled several of the highest official situations in Ireland and was ancestor of the Barons Mountmorris, Barons of Newport Pagnell, Viscounts Valentia and Lords Anglesey. He held 96,284 acres of forfeited estates in Beara and Bantry, and had a patent for the holding of fairs in Beara and Bantry.

Edward Eyre, of Galway, had large estates in that county and also in Cork and Kerry. He also seems to have been a money lender. He died before March 1739, having the previous year demised 102 acres of land in Leitrim, Co. Galway to Henry Puxley.

Of Edward Eyre's daughters: Margaret married Francis Annesley, of Ballysax, Co. Kildare, and on his death in 1751 she inherited a substantial portion of the Annesley's Beara estate, and married secondly Dominic Burke of Dublin, who died in 1785. She died in 1787.

Elizabeth Eyre married William Rowan of Stephenstown, Naas, and Richmond, Surrey, who died in 1768. She died in 1775. They had an only daughter Jane, who married Gavan Hamilton and was the mother of Archibald Hamilton Rowan.

Jane Eyre married her cousin Col. Samuel Eyre. The following is a brief abstract from 'The True Story of the Two Chiefs of Dunboy' :

> There they met Mr. John Rowan, who was agent to Francis Annesley, and William Rowan, joint owners in the right of their wives of a large estate in the neighbourhood and landlords of the O'Sullivans. Rowan, who lodged at the inn, was on friendly terms with the Puxleys.²

In Dublin, on 3 March 1722, Sir Richard Levinge married Mary Johnson. He died in 1724 and in November 1732 Dame Mary Levinge married Charles Annesley, who died in 1747, upon which Dame Mary came in for his portion of the Annesley estate.

About this time the male line of the Annesley family began to fade out, the sons showing a marked disinclination to marry, perhaps in reaction to the much marrying of their ancestors, especially their Uncle Richard, who never seemed quite sure who were his wives and who his mistresses! When Richard Annesley died in 1761, to say that his estates were in a mess would be to put it mildly. So too was the Lavallin estate when John Puxley (Copper John), founder of the family fortunes, saw his chance.

James Matthew Melchoir Lavallin was sued by Alicia O'Callaghan and paid £8,000 and costs. Phillip Lavallin of Carrigaline died in December 1700, having mortgaged his estate to Alicia O'Callaghan, the debt now amounting to £11,000. The estate was divided between two sisters, Sarah and Mary. Henry Puxley, son of John Puxley who was shot by Morty Oge O'Sullivan, married Mary and their son, John (Copper John) paid off all the debts and encumbrances and took over the entire Lavallin property. He also saw the opportunity of acquiring some of the Annesley lands, firstly by lease and then by purchase.

When John and Henry Puxley came to Beara in 1730 they were friendly with the O'Sullivans and aided them in many a smuggling venture. The principal import on these ventures was wine and the main export wool, so, as all the gentlemen on the coast liked their uncustomed wine and a profitable market for their wool, they connived at these smuggling enterprises.

However, in September 1732, Richard Tonson, customs officer for the Baltimore district, was storm-bound in Berehaven, and the rector, Rev. Waterhouse Sheppey, offered hospitality to him and his subordinates, Thomas Lucas, surveyor of Baltimore, and Henry King, hearth money collector. They accepted the invitation but it soon became evident that it was a trap laid by the Puxleys and O'Sullivans to assassinate three men who were becoming too much of a nuisance. However, the men escaped and Tonson and King managed to get to the barracks at Nedeen (Kenmare); Lucas became exhausted, but eventually reached a place of safety. A rift, which was to widen, appeared between the Puxleys and the O'Sullivans, as Puxley blamed Morty Oge for the escape from the rectory of the three king's officers. Moreover, in an argument about the affair, one Burke, a nephew of the Puxleys, shot one of the O'Sullivans.

Now from the end of the 1730s a new export took preference with Morty Oge, the export of men, most of them deserters from the army and navy who sought service in foreign armies. Henry Puxley, as land agent, employer of labour and lessee of lay tithes, could not possibly condone this new turn and, no doubt, there were frequent disagreements between him and Morty Oge on the subject. At the end of 1741 the Puxleys gathered around themselves a body of armed retainers, amongst whom were their nephews Walter FitzSimon and John Burke, and three Flahertys, while the O'Sullivans had many local supporters.

At the battle of Culloden where, incidentally, the officer in whom Bonnie Prince Charlie placed most trust was John William O'Sullivan from Kenmare, Morty Oge and John Puxley found themselves on opposite sides. There is a local tradition that Bonnie Prince Charlie, after landing in Donegal, came down the west coast of Ireland, no doubt with John William O'Sullivan, and that the French came in to Firkeel

Harbour, near Dursey, and took him back to France. The site of the house in which he is reputed to have stayed is still pointed out. (See Chapter 11.)

In 1752 John Puxley was appointed a Commissioner of the Peace and after that only his blood could satisfy Morty Oge. On 10 March 1754, the second Sunday in Lent, John Puxley, with his wife and family, set out for church. On their way they had to pass a forge kept by one Darby Harrington. In the forge that day were, in addition to Harrington, Morty Oge O'Sullivan, Little John Sullivan and Daniel Connell, as well as Morty Oge's brother-in-law, Henry Leary. And there John Puxley was shot dead.

The widow had now to rely on her husband's nephews, Henry FitzSimon and his brother Walter, who managed to have Harrington and Leary arrested. At the coroner's inquest Harrington made a confession and, later at the Assizes, both he and Leary were acquitted. On 29 March a proclamation was issued offering £200 reward for the capture of Morty Oge and £100 for each of his followers. Morty Oge was now ready to sail to France with 49 deserters from the British forces in Cork. On 30 March an order was sent to Sir William Boothby, commander of His Majesty's forces in Cork, to make plans for Morty Oge's capture and two days later he set out for Bantry with two companies of foot and made his way to Dunboy, where the unfortunate Mrs. Puxley had to entertain him for four days. But they had talked too long and Morty Oge was gone. Towards the end of April he sailed back into Kenmare Bay and anchored at Ballycrovane, near his house at Eyeries. But news of his return had reached Cork and, with great secrecy, an expedition to effect his capture was carefully planned.

Troops were brought down from Cork in hookers and kept well concealed and they succeeded in arriving at Eyeries without being observed. At Morty Oge's house the occupants were challenged and immediately replied, but torrential rain rendered the guns of the attackers useless, so FitzSimon offered a reward for anyone who would set fire to the house and this was duly done. The inhabitants now ran out of the house and were let pass by. The last three to emerge were Daniel Connell and Little John Sullivan, the flints of whose guns were so worn with firing they refused to go off, and they were captured; and then came Morty Oge, whose gun also failed to fire. A dozen muskets were fired at him: only one went off and that killed him. It was Sunday 5 May, eight weeks since John Puxley was shot.

In those days it was not a profitable thing to be on the side of law and order, Walter FitzSimon finding that not only had he to defray the legal expenses of the prosecution but he also had to tip the soldiers who guarded the gallows at the executions of Morty Oge's associates.

On 4 June 1754 Henry Puxley, son of John Puxley, entered Kilkenny School. He was born in 1741 and in July 1771 he married Sarah, daughter and co-heiress of Philip Lavallin of Waterstown Castle, Co. Cork, and was killed by a fall from his horse in 1803.

Henry's son (born 1772) was John Lavallin Puxley of Dunboy Castle and Llethr Llestri, Carmarthenshire, a Georgian mansion built in 1740 and purchased by him in 1797. He served as a Deputy Lieutenant for Carmarthenshire and in 1832 he became High Sheriff for that county. In 1796 he married Sarah Hobbes, who died 8 December 1831, daughter of Thomas Hobbes of Bantry, Co. Cork, and died 8 November 1856. His eldest son, Henry Lavallin Puxley, was born in 1797 and died unmarried on 13 June 1828.

In 1811 the attention of the above John Lavallin Puxley (grandson of the John Puxley who was shot by Morty Oge), was drawn to the fact that there was copper on his estate by Colonel S. C. Hall, who had served in a former regiment in which there were a number of Cornish miners. Puxley lost no time in getting some mining engineers over from Cornwall and having this confirmed. By deed dated 20 March 1812 he leased from Robert Hedges Eyre, of Macroom Castle, all Eyre's interests in 'all manners of mines, pits, veins of lead, copper ore, coals, culm, lapic calimarus, tin, iron, iron stone, cobalt, antimony, bismuth, and all other mineral ores and fossils now open and known, or to be found by digging, delving, sinking or otherwise in the lands of Coombe, Comminches, Clone owse, Cloune (Cluin), and Allihies, Barony of Bere and Bantry, Puxley to pay reasonable compensation to the tenants.'[3] The witnesses to the deed were Edward Puxley (illegitimate brother of John) and Francis Mealy. The period of the lease was 31 years and it was renewed by deed dated 7 December 1830.[4] And thus it was that John Lavallin Puxley got his sobriquet of 'Copper John'.

It is interesting that in a deed connected with the sale of some of the Galway lands, dated 19 November 1764 (Mary Puxley, Henry Puxley, John and Theobald Burke), one of the witnesses was 'Owen Sullivan, of Dorsey Island, yeoman', only 10 years after Henry's father was shot by an O'Sullivan.

Copper John had six daughters. Sarah was born in 1796 and died unmarried 8 May 1807. Elizabeth was life tenant of Lavallin House, Tenby, Pembrokeshire and Llethr Llestri, to which she succeeded under the terms of a trust formed by her father. She died unmarried in 1871, when the estates passed to her nephew, Rev. Herbert Boyne Lavallin Puxley. Copper John's third daughter, Barbara, died unmarried in 1842. His fourth daughter, Fanny, married Rev. Henry Herbert of Montgomeryshire, and had issue. The fifth daughter, Henrietta, married Robert Thomas, 10th Regiment and had issue. The sixth daughter, Jane,

95

died unmarried in 1829.

Copper John Puxley was succeeded by his younger son, John Lavallin Puxley, of Llethr Llestri, who was born in 1800, educated at Eton and Brasenose College, Oxford and in 1830 married Fanny Rosa Maria White, who died in 1857, daughter of Simon White of Glengarriff Castle, Co. Cork, and niece of the first earl of Bantry. This John Lavallin Puxley died, in his father's lifetime, on 23 October 1837.

He had two sons: John Simon Lavallin Puxley, of Dunboy Castle, Captain 6th Dragoons, born 18 July 1831, died unmarried, 15 April 1860. He was 'Wild Johnny' in *Hungry Hill*. The second son, Henry Lavallin Puxley, M.A., of Dunboy Castle, was J. P. in Cork and Carmarthenshire, and High Sheriff of Co. Cork 1865 and of Carmarthenshire in 1864. He was born 4 April 1834 and married, as his first wife, 4 June 1857, Katherine Ellen Waller, and succeeded his brother John in 1860.

Puxley's Mansion, Dunboy

He conceived the idea of building a Gothic extension to Dunboy and had plans for this drawn up by the architect John Christopher (1828-1910). The tender of the noted builders the Cockburns was accepted in July 1866 and building was commenced. The stone used was Ballyknockane (Co. Wicklow) granite faced with Ballintemple limestone. Christopher did not supervise the building of the new extension; this was the responsibility of the Dublin architect E. H. Carson, father of the controversial statesman Sir Edward Carson. In October 1867 the new building was roofed. Then it was agreed that the old building should be remodelled to fit in with the new, and, when the question of payment came up, this led to a dispute, the Puxleys assuming that it would be included in the general contract while the Cockburns, rather naturally, charged extra for it. The matter went to law but was eventually settled out of court.

In August 1872 Mrs. Puxley died in childbirth and was buried in the little cemetery in Adrigole, after which her husband left Ireland, never to return. The castle was let to various relatives of the Puxleys from time to time. Then in 1921 one Albert Thomas and his wife came as caretakers of Dunboy. He afterwards wrote his autobiography *Wait and See*, in which he gives an interesting account of their stay in Dunboy and the burning of the castle. When they arrived first at Dunboy there were two young naval officers staying there. These would have been Henry Waller Lavallin Puxley and John Paul Lavallin Puxley of whom anon.

The family of Henry Lavallin Puxley and his wife were:

(1) John Lavallin Puxley, born 21 September 1859, died unmarried 13 September 1896.

(2) Edward Lavallin Puxley, born 10 June 1861, died unmarried 3 December 1890.

(3) Henry Edmund Lavallin Puxley, born 14 February 1866 and married, 15 September 1897, Jane Eliza Halahan, only daughter of Rev. John Halahan. Henry Edmund died 13 August 1900, leaving two sons.

Henry Waller Lavallin Puxley, R. N., succeeded his grandfather in Dunboy Castle, which was burnt down by the I.R.A. in 1921 and sold in 1922. He was educated at the Royal Naval Colleges of Osborne and Dartmouth. He was born 27 June 1898 and married 20 July 1925 Naumai Kathleen Clephane Guinness, only daughter of Edwin Rowland Guinness of Timaru, New Zealand. He died in 1973 without issue.

His only brother, John Paul Lavallin Puxley, Lieutenant Commander, R.N., was born 25 January 1900, educated at the Royal Naval Colleges of Osborne and Dartmouth, married on 22 September 1956 Janet Agnes, daughter of Benjamin Mantle, of Jesmond, Biggleswade, Bedfordshire. He had no family and, consequently, on his death following a car accident at Christmas 1982 the Dunboy branch of the family ceased.

John Paul told me that, after his father's death, they spent the first six months of each year in Switzerland and the second six months with their grandparents at the Glebe, Castletownbere. Then, on 4 August 1909, their mother, Jane Eliza, married William Steele Haughton, M.D., of Dublin (who died 12 October 1951), after which their residence was in

Dublin. Jane Eliza died 10 September 1965, shortly after she paid her last visit to Dunboy. Commander Puxley said those six months spent in Berehaven were the happiest of his life.

In 1976 a friend wrote to me for some information on the facts, or otherwise, of the novel *Hungry Hill*. He had no conscious memory of hearing the name Puxley before and was not aware that the Puxleys and the family of Brodrick in the novel were the same family. My reply reminded him that when his father died in 1969 a medal case was found at the bottom of an old box and in this was an Oxford and Cambridge Rowing medal. He had no idea how it came into his father's possession but his father had worked for a number of years in a pawn shop until it closed down, and it is a fair assumption that it may have been given to him as a souvenir or part payment of wages. On receiving my letter my friend examined the medal more closely and found inscribed on the rim 'E. Lavallin Puxley 1884.' He then expressed a wish to give it back to the Puxley family and asked if I could arrange this. I duly made an appointment in England with Lieutenant Commander John Paul Lavallin Puxley and handed the medal over to him. We had a most interesting conversation and he confirmed that the medal had been won by his uncle Edward Lavallin Puxley (1866-1897).

As well as three sons Henry Lavallin Puxley, M.A., (1834-1909) had three daughters:

(1) Maria Frances, married 20 March 1884, as his second wife, Robert O'Brien Studdert J. P. of Cullane, Co. Clare. She died 15 July 1919, leaving issue, and he died 31 January 1936.

(2) Katherine Rosa married her cousin, Simon White of Glengarriff Castle, and had issue.

(3) Elizabeth Jane born 1872, died unmarried 1936. She was 'poor lame Lizette' who lived at Glengarriff Castle and looked after the White children.

It was said of Maria Frances that she married Robert O'Brien Studdert to get away from her step-mother!

Henry Lavallin Puxley married secondly, 9 December 1875, Adeline, widow of Colonel William Ferguson Hutchinson and youngest daughter of General Charles W. Nepean, nephew of Sir Evan Nepean, 1st bart, and died 6 February 1909.

According to *Burke's Landed Gentry,* the principal member of the family would in 1970 appear to be Major John Philip Lavallin Puxley, T.D., of Llethr Llestri, Carmarthenshire, and Welford Park, Berkshire, solicitor, who had issue James Henry Lavallin Puxley born 23 October 1948, educated Eton College and Bristol University (B.A. 1970) and Charles John Lavallin Puxley, commanded Royal Green Jackets 1970, born 20 August 1950. Other branches of the family are widely scattered: Quebec, Ottawa, Islington, Ontario, Halifax, Nova Scotia, Uxbridge, Ontario, St. Johns, New Brunswick, Sydney, Australia, Toronto, Canada, and, in England, Surrey and Berkshire.

Whatever inspiration Beara may have had for novelists it does not seem to have extended to Christian names for, as we have seen, Standish O'Grady used the Christian names of his own family, and Froude, in his *Two Chiefs of Dunboy*, appears to have changed few names, that of Puxley (Colonel Goring), Vallancy (Vavasour) and the keeper of the forge at Dunboy, whom he calls Minahan. Froude also retains unaltered place names and the name of Morty Oge O'Sullivan's boat, the *Doutelle*. Incidentally, Froude's account of the scene in the forge places Morty Oge in a better light than does the official government report.

If one compares the genealogy 'Puxley of Dunboy Castle' in *Burke's Landed Gentry* with characters in the novel *Hungry Hill* by Daphne du Maurier, it will be found that the Christian names of the Brodrick family in the novel agree with the Christian names of the Puxley family in *Burke's Landed Gentry*. The names of places have been changed, but not to such an extent as to make them unidentifible. Moreover, other identifications of places and people can be made from mines records, parish registers, family traditions and printed sources. The recollections of descendants of the families concerned agree remarkably with local traditions, though this may arise from people having read the book, but in some cases it seems unlikely.

The following would appear to be the places and people of *Hungry Hill*:

Andriff	=	Glengarriff
Doonhaven	=	Berehaven
Doon Island	=	Bere Island
Slane	=	Cork
Mundy	=	Bantry
Clonmere	=	Dunboy
Bronsea	=	Swansea
Ardmore	=	Adrigole
Duncroom	=	Macroom
Lletharrog	=	Llethr Llestri
Saunby	=	Tenby
Denmare	=	Kenmare
Oakmount	=	Oakmount
Kileen	=	u n i d e n t i f i e d , somewhere on the road to Kenmare, perhaps

		Ardgroom, where the Puxleys had property.
Brodrick	=	Puxley
Copper John Brodrick	=	Copper John Puxley
Donovans	=	Donegans
Robert Lumley	=	Robert Hedges Eyre, of Macroom, from whom Puxley leased mining rights.
Lord Mundy	=	Lord Bantry
Rev. Tom Callaghan and his wife Harriet	=	Rev. John Halahan and his wife Harriet
Simon Flower	=	Simon White, brother of Lord Bantry
Fanny Rosa Flower	=	Fanny Rosa Maria White, daughter of Simon White
Boles	=	Major Charles W. Bowlby
Hare	=	Wm. Hare, Viscount Ennismore, grandson of the Earl of Listowel, and M.P. Co. Kerry 1829.
Kate Donovan	=	Ellen Donegan, the birth of whose illegitimate daughter, Ellen, by John L. Puxley is registered in the Protestant Church, Castletownbere 1860.
Robert O'Brien Spencer,	=	Robert O'Brien J. P. Studdert, J. P. Cullane, Co. Clare
Adeline Price	=	Adeline, 2nd wife of Henry L. Puxley

A couple of hundred metres to the east of the mansion of Dunboy will be found the O'Sullivan Beare castle, site of the famous siege of 1602. Excavation has revealed that this was much more extensive than was originally thought and that it had been partially rebuilt as a Cromwellian star-shaped fort.

There are two detailed contemporary accounts of the circumstances

Ruins of Dunboy Castle

and events of the siege. Sir George Carew's version is given in Thomas Stafford's *Pacata Hibernia* (London, 1633), Standish O'Grady edition (London: Downey & Co., 1896). The viewpoint of the defenders of Dunboy appears in Don Philip O'Sullivan Beare's *Historiae Catholicae Iberniae* (Lisbon, 1621), translated by Matthew J. Byrne as *A History of Ireland under Elizabeth* (Dublin: Sealy, Bryers and Walker, 1903).

SKETCH-MAP OF ALLIHIES AREA

TOWNLANDS

1. Tilickafinna
2. Kilmichael
3. Ballynacallagh
4. Ballaghboy
5. Billeragh
6. Garinish
7. Ballynacarriga
8. Glanarough
9. Canalmore
10. Scrivoge
11. Loughanamore
12. Cloghfune
13. Killough West
14. Killough East
15. Ballydonegan
16. Kilkinnikin West
17. Reentrusk

18. Allihies
19. Cloan
20. Caminches
21. Kealoge
22. Cahermeelabue
23. Kilkinnikin East
24. Knockroe West
25. Loughane Beg
26. Coom
27. Part of Knockroe West
28. Knockroe Middle
29. Knockroe East
30. Canalough
31. Lickbarrahane
32. Cloghane Lower
33. Cloghane Upper
34. Garranes
35. Brackcloon

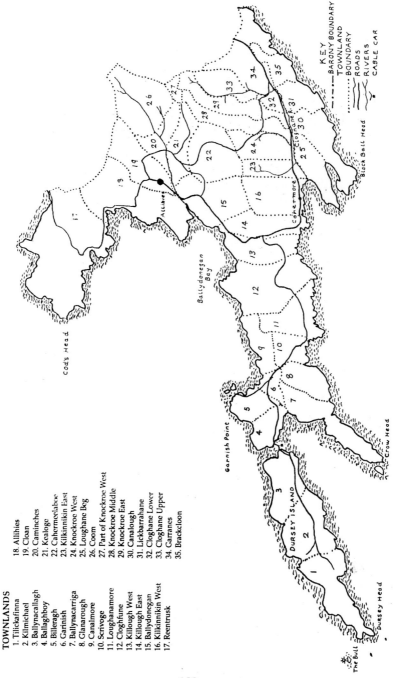

102

Chapter 11

Dunboy to Dursey

Continuing on westward by the main road from the gate of Dunboy, the road sweeps up to the Gap of Gour. In the curve of the road, to the southeast will be seen a slim standing stone, measuring 2.15m by .70m by .15m. It is marked on the Ordnance Survey map as 'Gallaun' and is site 96 on the Berehaven list. It is mentioned by Thomas Johnson Westropp in his list of 'The Promontory Forts of Beare and Bantry,' as 'the Gour ogmic stone, with its pathetic epitaph "Cari".' [1] There is now no trace of this inscription (Westropp was writing in 1921) and he also refers to 'the seven blue lakelets of Pulleen', of which there are now not more than three or four left.

There is a splendid view from here, looking back up Bantry Bay, and on passing westward through the gap, an equally fine seascape lies ahead. Just beyond the gap a lane leads in from the left which provides some good walks. Around the next corner, where the road has been widened to facilitate rounding a very sharp bend, turn left. Stop at the second house on the righthand side of the road: opposite there is a stile crossing the fence and a streamlet, and in the next small field to the south will be found site 109 Brackloon, which is not marked on the Ordnance Survey map. It is a rock-cut souterrain, or at least it was so written up by the late Professor S. P. Ó'Ríordáin, in the *Journal of the Irish Naturalist* (vol. 5), but in recent years there has been rethinking on this, some archaeologists suggesting that it may be an ordinary souterrain from over which the associated fort has been eroded, while others consider that it may have been an iron smelting site. My opinion, for what it is worth, is that it was a corn drying kiln.

Continuing along this road, the next turn to the right down a steep hill with sharp bends takes one back to the main road at Knockroe Bridge, east of the old Cahermore school. Here we see the wild coastline stretching away to Dursey Island, with the little harbour of Black Ball at Loughanbeg and the prominent headland of that name in the foreground.

On this headland is a square watch tower enclosed by a circular wall and there is a narrow grassy field running up towards the tower. The field does look like a road of the Napoleonic period and the buildings are regarded as being of that period too. However, in 1632 the Lord President St. Leger ordered beacons

to be set up at Cape Clear, Mizen Head, Sheep Head, Dursey,

Berehaven, Great Island (Bere Island) and other places for defence against Turkish Pirates. Mr. Daniel O'Sullivan has a house of reasonable strength at Berehaven and takes on himself to defend it and Ballygobbin; he promises to erect five beacons — one upon the Durseys and four upon the Great Island.[2]

There were four martello towers on Bere Island, Rerrin and Ardaragh, which were destroyed to make room for other fortifications, Ardagh and Clonaghlin. Captain T. M. Keogh says: 'The so-called Princess Beara's Castle was constructed at the same time as a signal or look-out tower, communicating with similar buildings whose ruins may be seen near Sheep's Head, on Dursey Island, and on Blackball Head.'[3] In 1810 the following four leases of land on Bere Island for the purpose of building fortifications were signed:

11 May 1810, Robert Hedges of Macroom and Thos. Lahy of Cork to Brig Gen Benjamin Fisher and Brig Gen Thomas Trotters, Ordnance Department.
No. 2 as above but mentions 'Goggin's Lot'.
No. 3 as above but dated 11 January 1810.
No. 4 as above but undated, Daniel O'Sullivan of Castletown, Murtogh O'Sullivan of Coulagh and John Lavallin Puxley, of Llbetherlieseley to Brig Gen Benjamin Fisher and Brig Gen Thomas Trotters.

Martello Tower

In 1694, on 19 October, orders were issued from the Lords Justices and Monsieur Cust, Lieut. of Ordnance, for a survey of Bantry Bay to decide on the most suitable place for fortification: the report, 'Memoir et Reflections sur la construction d'un ou deux forts a la baye de Bantry', chose Berehaven.

In 1705 General Ingoldsby visited the southwest coast of Ireland to seek suitable harbours for fortification.

In view of this it seems probable that the square towers were built at an earlier date than the martellos.

Owing to the names of the coves on each side of Black Ball Head, Bunnadoonroe and Coosbunnadoonroe, the scattered rocks and general character of the platform, Thomas Johnson Westropp considered that there is the strongest case for regarding it as the site of a headland fort, *Dún Rua* (the red fort). This area is in the townland of Canalough.

On the western side of Black Ball Head is the site of an extinct volcano and asbestos may be found here, also other volcanic rock.

At Knockroe Bridge near the main road there is a sign for Loughanbeg Pier. Follow this road down to Black Ball Harbour. This is the best point from which to climb up and explore Black Ball Head, and also on the other side of the harbour there is White Ball Head, where a short walk can be worthwhile. On this little peninsula there is a natural arch, Poulnaglass, a natural hole in the ground, and an inaccessible cave, and on a stormy day the white foam blowing up through Poulnaglass and Thunderbolt Hole can be very spectacular.

The area was once thickly populated, and tradition says that among those who lived here were people named Griffin who came from Kerry and others named Spring who paid girls four pence a day to collect seaweed. There is a long quite substantial wall, said to have been a row of houses. The end one was the best; it was known as the White House and was where the landlord stayed when he came to collect the rent.

To the east of Knockroe Bridge close to the river there is one small archaeological site which should be visited, if only because I searched for it on and off over a period of 10 years and, in spite of the fact that it is marked on the map as 'Gallaun', failed to find it. I am grateful to Mrs. Bennie Hanley for pointing out the fallen stone in the spring of 1980.

Here there is so much to be seen it is difficult to know where to start. From Knockroe Bridge back along the main road towards Castletownbere for 1.5 km, take the next turn sharp left (signposted to Allihies). A few hundred metres up the road is the first turn to the right. Go up this road for about three fields and three fields in from the road on the right will be found site 175 Cloghane Upper. It consists of a ringwall enclosure, not very well built and without any sign of a fosse. It has a diameter of 20m and the walls are 1.25m high. To the southwestern side of the ringwall a small diamond-shaped field or enclosure is attached to it. Southeast of this monument is a boulder burial, not marked on the Ordnance Survey map. The boulder measures 2.70m by 2m by .80m and rests on the usual three supporting stones, there being a pegstone between the boulder and one of the supporters to keep it in place. When we were first surveying this site a bull came along to see what we were up to, but decided it was all rather boring and peacefully departed.

Returning to the upper main road to Allihies, turn right and continue for about 300m and take the first branch road to the right and this will, a similar distance up, join a road back to the main road. This is Caheraphuca and the 'fort of the pooka' will be found in the angle between the two roads and south of them. It is marked on the Ordnance Survey six inch map as 'Caheraphuca' and is set on a shallow precipice over a small stream, with a good view seawards over Black Ball and White Ball heads. It is, however, very much ruined, most of the bank having fallen into the stream below. This is site 98 and is in the townland of Knockroe East, as is No. 99, just south of and across the main Allihies road, in the first field to the west and behind an outhouse. It is a large standing stone, about 3m long by 1m wide and has fallen onto a smaller standing stone, both stones being incorporated into a modern field fence. It is southwest of Caheraphuca and in a line with site 97 over the old Cahermore school.

From Caheraphuca westwards the route is of more scenic than archaeological interest so we will return, east and west, to Knockroe Bridge on the lower main road to Allihies. Just after the old Cahermore school, turn right into a space where there is a shop and post office. Here take the path leading uphill to the right. After a very short distance the path turns left into a field where to the east will be found site 97. This is a fine ex-standing stone, marked on the map as 'Gallaun'. It is almost 3m high by 1.50m wide. Coming down from Canalough in 1967 I was saddened to find it was no longer towering up on the hill behind the school. A local man told me it had fallen after exceptionally heavy rain, the night, as he put it, 'after the all-Ireland final'. Yet even in its debased state it is of interest, for one can now see the quite large pegstone that held it in position, and how very little of the stone was actually under ground.

A short distance west of here, a couple of fields up the road on the left, a gate leads into the left where there is a ford over the shallow Cloghane River. From here a laneway leads southwards to a gap on the lefthand side and inside this will be found site 107. This is probably a ring fort, but, once again, it is unlike most ring forts around here both in its flatness and its positioning, and there is a very slight possibility that it may be a Norman moated grange.

Along the ridge of high ground running westward, north of and more or less parallel to the main Castletownbere-Dursey road, from Knockroe West to Kilkinnahan West are a line of five small ring forts, sites 102, 103, 104, 105 and 106. These are of no special interest, and are not too easy of access though there are very narrow rough tracks leading up to most of them from the lower main road, and to some of them from the upper main road.

We continue along the lower main road through Cahermore, with the church on high ground to the right. Approximately 1 km further on past the church, take the first road to the left, which plunges steeply down into the valley and just as steeply up the other side. Off this a lane runs in left to site 110 Killough West, a killeenagh on a rise 80m along the lane in a field on the right. On the map there is a fort, marked as 'Killeenagh Burial gd disused'. It was overgrown but we were able to see the headstones. The presence of these stones indicates that it was, at one time, a monastic settlement.

As we have seen in Chapter 8, in the Decretal Letter of Pope Innocent III, the four parishes west of Bantry are given as Cellechdach (Killeacac or Killough), Cellmana (Kilmanagh or Allihies), Cellchattigern (Kilcatherine) and Cellmoceogain (Kilmackowen). Undoubtedly this place is the Cellechdach (church of the miracles) or Killough of Pope Innocent's Decretal Letter though, like Canon John Lyons, I have failed to find reference to it elsewhere.

We return to the main road and continue on about 200m to Barness Gap where the road goes straight on to Allihies and the turn for Dursey is on the left. Close to the junction, on the left below the road, is a very fine wedge grave, site 101 Killough East. The capstone measures 3.20m long by .70m thick, and the side stones measure 3m long by .70m by .15m, and 1.40m long by .20m by .40m. Two large slabs rest against the southern end of the tomb and it is possible there may have been a second chamber. On the capstone there are small circular depressions like cup-marks but they are rather crude and it is probable that they are merely weathering.

There was a tradition that two giants fought at this gap and killed each other. I used to imagine that these two giants were really two ice floes, one coming down Bantry Bay and one bursting through Barness Gap from the Kenmare ice cap, meeting head-on and destroying each other. But, alas for my fancies, in road-widening work here about 1960 another stone-lined chamber was found under the ground, and, unfortunately, destroyed before it could be inspected. Earlier still another chamber was similarly destroyed at the Gap of Gour.

A cottage in the curve below the road level used to be pointed out in

Wedge tomb, Killough (site 101)

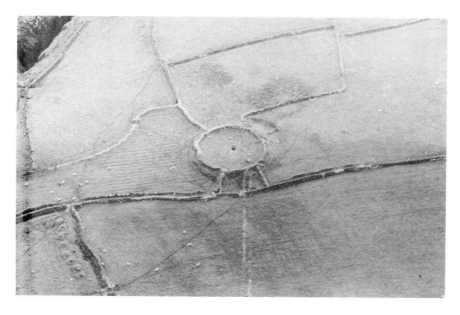

Ring fort, Lehanmore (site 113)

recent years as the home of the faint-hearted Reiry O'Sullivan Beare in 1581.

In 1641 these lands of Killaghagh, or Killough, belonged to Donagh O'Sullivan Beare, and, with the O'Donegan lands of Carrownidonegan, Kilmannah, and Knockalgoural, made up the parish of Kilmannah and were estimated at 2½ quarters, paying 40/- to the MacCarthy More and £4 13s 4d to O'Sullivan Beare. The Donegans, with the Lynches, were a small clan but an extremely ancient one. There were a number of tribes of this name throughout the country such as those in north Cork, north Tipperary, Co. Monaghan, Co. Roscommon and Co. Westmeath, but it would appear that none of them were related.

In many cases the old parish boundaries give us the limits of the old septs or clans, and were, in fact, the still older tuaths (territories) adopted to an ecclesiastical use.

Take the Dursey road. (An alternative route to the abovementioned killeenagh is to take the very sharp first turn to the left, and about 100m down is the lane to the right.) Continue on to Lehanmore (Loughanemore), where on 8 November 1897 Rev. Michael MacCarthy of Allihies leased a plot of ground for a teacher's house at a rent of two pence per year for 91 years.

When we get to the shop and community centre at Lehanmore there will be seen, near the cliff edge to the south, a ring fort. The wall of this is in good condition, but the fosse has largely disappeared and the entrances to the souterrain, both within and without the fort, have been filled up. A place about 2m east of the fort was pointed out to me as where the souterrain entrance had been. This is site 113 in the Berehaven list.

Continuing west of Lehanmore community centre, the road runs along a cliff top giving fine views of Firkeel Bay, Foilnaman, Horn Point and the intriguingly named Stallion's Creek. To the west the land runs out southwards in a peninsula to Crow Head and Crow Island, the latter, from this angle, being indistinguishable from the mainland. Some time ago a local man built his own cable car from the mainland to Crow Island.

To the south of Crow Head a patch of foam will be seen at most stages of the tide and except in the calmest of weather. This indicates the Cat Rock, beyond the west extremity of Crow Island. About 290m to the westward of Crow Island lies the Bull's Forehead under about 1.2m of water. Yet another rock, Old Breaker, with 9.6m over it, lies about midway between the inner part of Crow Head promontory and Illanebeg, the southeast part of Dursey Island. It is possible to pass through here into Dursey Sound in calm weather but it is extremely dangerous. Froude uses this place for an incident in his novel *The Two*

Chiefs of Dunboy, when Morty Oge O'Sullivan in his little vessel, the *Doutelle*, is being rapidly overtaken by the much larger and faster English frigate, the *Aeolus*, and he escapes through this dangerous passage into Dursey Sound and Kenmare Bay, thence to Derrynane. Froude knew his navigation and apparently he knew the coastline as well, for not only does he write a graphic and exciting tale but an accurate one too. In 1941 the famous yachtsman Conor O'Brien used this passage for an incident in his novel *The Runaways*.

There is a tradition that a blacksmith named the 'Gullawn Gow' lived on Crow Island. There were a lot of stories told about him which, unfortunately, I have forgotten, but one old man said that he was a 'fifth columnist' who was making swords and spears, 'for the Danes'!

But to return to our viewpoint on the mainland beyond Lehanmore: there is a short lane leading up to the right to a farm and the same old man pointed out a thatched cabin at the end of the lane and said, 'Some kind of a king or prince was running away after a battle in a place called Calladen (sic) in Scotland and he stayed in that cabin until the French came in to Firkeel Harbour and took him to France.'

As the road passes through Firkeel Gap a branch road runs down left to Firkeel village and harbour, while another runs up to the right to Canalmore, both of them being cul-de-sacs. Below Canalmore on the southern shore of Garinish Bay there is site 173, a semi-circular enclosure on the cliff edge over the little inlet of Faill an Uisce. It almost certainly is a promontory fort but we have not managed to get down to survey it, and that expert on promontory forts, Thomas Johnson Westropp, does not include it in 'The Promontory Forts of Beara and Bantry'.

On passing through Firkeel Gap one comes out on the northern side of the peninsula, overlooking Kenmare Bay and the Kerry mountains, a very fine view. The first road to the right leads down to two sandy and very safe bathing beaches and between them is a stony strand. The road ends at Garinish quay and boat slip. Here are Little Island, Long Island and Garinish Island. The sea in stormy weather breaks over these islands and makes a most impressive scene.

Return back uphill to rejoin the Dursey road, turn right towards Dursey and after about 200m turn left. The road zigzags upwards for about 400m, before it starts downhill. About here will be seen a small group of megalithic monuments, which comprise site 114 Ballynacarriga. To the right, just inside the road fence, is a boulder burial. The boulder capstone measures 2.50m by 1.80m by .60m, running north and south. It rests on the usual three supporting boulders. About 3.50m east of this is another boulder, well built into the wall between the road and the field. It is almost certainly another boulder burial but its position prevents measurements being taken, nor is it possible to see if it rests on supports

Boulder burial, Ballynacarriga (site 114)

or not. Across the road, in a field to the southeast, is a diamond-shaped boulder measuring 1.70m by 2.30m by .90m. It rests on three supporting stones and is undoubtedly another boulder burial. In the same field, 35m southeast of this dolmen is a low circular mound of an indeterminate nature, perhaps a housing site. There are also a couple of piles of small stones, but these are almost certainly field clearance.

Site 151 was another boulder dolmen in this area, but it was discovered some time after the above, and is two fields to the northeast of them. The boulder in this case measured 1.85m by 1.30m by .15m. Sad to relate, this dolmen was removed in field clearance about 1979. In the adjoining field is a rectangular house site, probably medieval.

This road is a cul-de-sac, so we must return to the Firkeel-Dursey road and turn to the left down to Dursey Sound. About 350m along on the right is a graveyard (so marked on the map) but, on closer inspection, this proves to be a ringwall enclosure and I was informed by a local man that there was a chamber under it in which the children used to play when he was a child and his father closed up the entrance lest some of the children might get trapped down there. The ringwall enclosure, traces of a fosse and the souterrain are all strong indications that the place was not only a fort but a monastic one. It is site 174. Continue on to the end of the road for the landing place and cable car for Dursey Island.

On the island there is a chapel in ruins, a burial ground, with a vault,

111

and on the island of Illanebeg is a fort and between this little island and Dursey itself is the site of a drawbridge. Further in on Dursey is a holy well at Ballynacallagh and further in still, at Kilmichael, is another church in ruins. These are marked on the Ordnance Survey map, but I have never managed to accomplish an archaeological survey of Dursey Island.

Chapter 12

Allihies Mines

We now return to Barness Gap and turn left through it. Some holes in the sides of the hills here, and in other parts of the peninsula, are indicative of early mining efforts. They are dangerous and should not be entered. On coming through Barness Gap to the northern side of the peninsula, a magnificent view will be had of Ballydonegan Bay, Allihies and the Kerry mountains, also of the Scariff islands and the Skelligs. Of Ballydonegan the Admiralty Sailing Instruction for 1887 has the following to say:

> Ballydonegan Bay, 2¼ miles east of Garinish, would, from its exposed and dangerous character, be unworthy of notice, excepting to warn the seaman against too near an approach to it, were it not the shipping port for the produce of the Berehaven copper mines. By the help of heavy moorings laid in the eastern bight of the bay, partially sheltered from the Atlantic swell by a few outlying rocks, the fine schooners belonging to the mining company are enabled to ship their cargoes, but no stranger should attempt to go near it. When caught by a northwest gale, the schooners have no resource but to ride it out at the moorings, the crew escaping in boats, and leaving the vessel to her fate.[1]

At the foot of the hill down from Barness a laneway runs in to the left and about 1 km along is Dooneen Point, site 79, a much destroyed promontory fort hardly worth going in to see. Continuing past the laneway turn, the road crosses a bridge and a little further on a shaft of a disused copper mine runs out to sea. A few hundred metres further on a little stream flows under the road over a waterfall, down to which a narrow path leads, rather steeply. Beyond this, on the lefthand side of the road, a gated track leads northwards into a field and here will be found site 111. It is marked on the Ordnance Survey map as 'Killeenagh (burial gd) disused' and this is what it undoubtedly is, but a rather unusual one. It is a ringwall enclosure, 8.40 m in diameter by 1.10m high. The earth within the ringwall rises higher than the outside ground level, almost to the top of the ringwall. On the northern side there are traces of a bank, 1.40m wide, which has been eroded around the rest of the ringwall. The headstones are few and small. The whole site is included in a modern fence. Adjoining this, to the south, is a circular patch in the ground showing where a ring fort once had been and, no doubt, the two are associated; perhaps a monastic settlement of short-lived duration or the home of a landowner, with the ringwall enclosure for his chaplain, later turned into a graveyard.

To our left here is Ballydonegan Strand, a high bank of sand, behind which a river flows down to the sea. The coarse sand is in fact the residue of the copper grindings from the Allihies mines. The strand is in a beautiful setting, an enjoyable place in which to relax, and a splendid place for children to play and explore, especially behind the river bank. The beach shelves very quickly, and if the sea is at all rough there is an undertow. There are three roads leading to Ballydonegan Strand. Keeping along the road we are on we come to Ballydonegan Bridge. Before the bridge there is a road down to the left; at the bridge there is a road running through a shallow river, with stepping stones, and a road straight on. The first two take one to the river behind the sandbank, and the one going straight on leads to the seaward side of the beach, from where another road runs northward, parallel to the coast, to join the main Allihies-Eyeries road a few hundred metres up at Dooneen. From Ballydonegan Bridge the main road runs up to the village of Allihies. Halfway between the bridge and the village a road runs to the left to join the abovementioned Ballydonegan-Dooneen road and on a straight stretch of this connecting road the boundary wall, at one point, curves in to avoid a large boulder resting on the ground. This is known as 'the landing place of the children of Lir' and it was said people used to 'make rounds' here and put money under the rock. When we first saw it this pecuniary store was reduced to one penny!

The two kings of the Tuath Dé Danann were Lir and Bove. Lir had two sons and two daughters. Their mother died and their father married a daughter of King Bove. She became jealous of the love King Lir had for his children and turned them into swans, condemning them to spend 300 years on the ice-cold waters of Lake Darvra in Westmeath, 300 years on the sea of Moyle between Scotland and Ireland, and the last 300 years in the Atlantic waters on Ireland's western coast, until the coming of St. Patrick. This last is the controversal one!

There are many places that claim the honour of their return to human form and acceptance of Christianity, such as Murlough Bay, Co. Antrim (this on the strength of gigantic footprints to be seen there but can hardly be said to be on the western coast), and between Erris Head and Inish Glora, both places near Belmullet, Co. Mayo.

We have seen the local tradition, and John O'Donoghue, describing his visit to Dursey, in *In a Quiet Land* says, 'Away to the west lay the three black and dangerous rocks called the Bull, the Cow and the Calf, around which the Children of Lir were said to have spent 300 years before the coming of St. Patrick.'[2] Then, of course, this area was among the first to accept Christianity in Ireland. Lir is confused frequently with Manannán Mac Lir, who was a much earlier personage, and had by this time become a god to the Tuatha Dé Danann. Lir was an ocean god in early Irish and British legend, and was probably the son of Don. He appears in Geoffrey of Monmouth's *Historia Britonum* as Leir, founder of the city of Leicester, and was the inspiration for Shakespeare's King Lear. He appears in the Mabinogion as 'Llyr'.

In the battle of Slieve Mish between the Milesians and the Tuatha Dé Danann, Scotta, wife of Milidh, was killed and was buried in Gleann na Scoithin, townland of Clahane, parish of Annagh, barony of Troughanamy, where her megalithic tomb may still be seen. Another victim, Ir, was buried on the Skelligs, where his tomb similarly survives. Also fell Fas, who is buried in Gleann Faisi, now Glenofaush, townland of Knockalee, barony of Ballycashlane. Don was buried on the Bull Rock.

In a map made by Janson of Amsterdam in 1670, the Skelligs appear as 'Middle Skellock and Great Skellock', while the Cow appears in one map as 'Torone' and in another as 'Towne'. The Calf appears as 'Grelagh' and the Bull Rock as 'Mosalah' or 'Mokologh'. It was sometimes called Inish Bui or Inis Bai. Before that it was known as *Teach Don*, 'the house of Don'. There is an arched cavern reaching through the Bull Rock. Don was god of the underworld and this arch was said to be the entrance to that world and he was waiting there to welcome those who had departed from this world. Another Milesian of interest to this area was Lugaid, son of Ith, ancestor to the O'Driscolls.

This great amphitheatre of Allihies, and, to a lesser extent, that of Eyeries to the north, is a rich copper-bearing area. The mineral was certainly worked in prehistoric times and, possibly, in the medieval period. The prehistoric mines usually consisted of an overhanging cliff or cave with quartz in the roof. A fire was lit beneath this quartz until it was thoroughly heated and then water was thrown on the quartz, causing it to break away from the parent mass of rock. The copper was then hammered and crushed with round sea stones until it parted from the quartz. Of course, as time went on, improvements were developed and I still feel annoyed with myself when I think of a nicely shaped stone that I once picked up at Allihies, admired and then threw away. It was only when I saw a similar one in the museum that I realized it was a maul used in the early working of copper. After this many were the searches I made for it, but, alas, without success! Near where I found it was a shallow, only inches deep, trough, lined with flat stones, and it was probably in this that the quartz was crushed.

In a report, dated 14 September 1691, from London to the Nunziatura di Fiandra, it was stated that a grant had been made recently to Joseph Horne and others to form a corporate body under the title 'Copper Miners of England' and that they had acquired a place in Ireland and in New England by permission of William and Mary.[3] It seems unlikely that the mines in Berehaven were worked then owing to the difficult terrain here. There were mines at Hollyford, Co. Tipperary, in 1850 and in these were found signs of earlier working, while the nearby copper mines of Oola were working in the year 1292. Other copper areas where the metal was comparatively easy to extract were in Co. Wicklow and Co. Waterford.

The extent of the mines at Allihies will be obvious from the number of shafts, chimneys, reservoirs and pumping stations around. As we have seen in Chapter 10, the presence of copper here was first pointed out in 1811 to the landowner John Puxley by Colonel Hall. The mines were opened in 1812 and in 1813 157 tons of ore was exported, and for the following years the exports were as follows:

1835	7,466 tons	of remarkably good ore	
1836	6,418 tons	valued at	£74,879 18s 0d
1840	4,808 tons	valued at	£40,981 2s 6d
1843	4,446 tons	valued at	£36,348 6s 0d
1855	5,227 tons	valued at	£56,580 0s 0d
1856	6,097 tons	valued at	£60,587 0s 0d
1863	8,573 tons		

When the mines were first opened they were called Allihies Mines, but the title was changed when the operations moved further afield and it was then called the Berehaven Mining Company.

In 1822 the mines gave constant employment to about 600 persons of both sexes, of all ages from 10 years upwards. The monthly expenditure was from £900 to £1,000 and the mine produced from 150 to 200 tons of ore. Lady Chatterton, in *Rambles in the South of Ireland*, gives the following description of these mines:

1838. The mines are now far from being so productive as formerly. The Company by which they are worked is at present going to great expense in a search, hitherto unavailing, after a new vein, and if the information of one of the captains is correct, they are now losing money. This account, however, is at variance with the stated produce; formerly it amounted to about 600 tons a month; now it averages 350 tons. Copper ore is worth £9 per ton, but the purchaser always takes off 2½ % a ton to cover their risk; consequently the real price is £7 10s 0d a ton; this at the former rate of production would give £54,300 a year,

116

and at the reduced rate of supply would give £31,500 a year. An eighth goes amongst the owners of the fee, four, I think, in number; formerly the principal one received £4,000 a year. The company's shares amount to 64 which are divided, I am told, between five proprietors, of whom Mr. Puxley, whose place we passed today, is the chief.

The works, it is said, employ 1000 people. Girls who attend to the washing of the ore get 3½ d a day, boys 6d, men from a shilling to 1s 4d. Miners work by task work; a gang undertakes a piece of work at so much per ton, the price being fixed by a master, the ore to produce 10%, to ascertain which an assay office is established. There are four captains. The men are paid monthly, and the calculation is made so as to give the men who handle powder 1s 4d a day, the others about 1s. The mine is about 110 fathoms deep, and they are working it deeper. Five steam engines are employed; the first we saw works the crushing machine and pounders. Over the pounded ore water is passed, the ore is then sifted, and, after a number of successive washings the dross is separated.

The situation of the head captain, as the principal miner is termed, is worth about £300 a year which includes his house and perquisites.[4]

An analysis of the ore showed it was composed of:

Copper	10.2%
Iron	10.8%
Sulphur	14.8%
Quartz	63.9%
Loss	0.3%
	100.0%

In 1845 the number employed was about 1000:

Miners	400
Smiths & Joiners	30
Helpers	25
Labourers	245
Boys	170
Girls	130 [5]

According to Robert Kane's 1845 account:

The most productive veins were the Mountain, which is about 450 feet above the level of the sea, on a large east and west lode and the Caminche vein, which runs north and east. From the Mountain mine a great quantity of copper has been raised and in 1845 they were still obtaining about 200 tons a month of about 10% produce. The principal working is about 760 feet in length and 852 feet in depth. The Caminche is worked for about 570 feet in length and 912 in depth. The engine shaft sinks 60 feet more. [6]

There were numerous other smaller mines in the area, such as Dooneen, Barness and Kealoge, and on the northern slopes of Knockoura Mountain there was the Marion mine. There are some half dozen shafts here and a couple of tunnels. The Marion mine may possibly have been named after Maria Frances Puxley, who married Robert O'Brien Studdert in 1884, but the workings do look earlier than that period.

About 1978 the late Mr. Herbert O'Sullivan of Allihies told me that a visitor to Allihies told him that his father had been an engineer in these mines and had said that in the mine there was a lake, upon which was a boat. This was confirmed by Mr. Bennie Hanley whose grandfather worked there and had said there was a flat-bottomed boat on the lake.

The mining company owned the following schooners: *Catherine Ellen* (Captain Harte) and *Henrietta* (Captain David Tamblyne). Other captains were Batt, Supple, Roycroft and Atteridge, but some of these may have been mines captains. In 1853 the following were mines captains: John Mack Reed, William Reed, John Reed, Superintendent, Matt Sylvester and Joseph Martin.

The Reeds had the reputation of being very good workers and there was in Allihies an expression to describe a hard-working man, 'He dug and delved like a Reed.' The Reeds worked on the principle of driving the main mine shaft deep and running small tunnels horizontally from it. Somebody suggested to the Puxleys that it would be quicker and cheaper to get the copper out if they enlarged these horizontal tunnels near the surface. John Puxley ordered the Reeds to do this but they refused, saying that, if they did, the mines would flood. Puxley insisted that they carry out his order, but the Reeds handed in their resignations rather than do something that would injure their reputations as miners. The incoming captain carried out Puxley's instructions and the mines flooded.

In 1867 and 1877 Henry Pascoe was manager of the Berehaven

Mines. In 1859 a Captain John Pascoe was manager of the copper mines at Hollyford, Co. Tipperary.

On 28 October 1869 a new joint stock company, the Mining Company of Ireland, was formed to purchase the Berehaven Mining Company. Its capital was 60,000 shares of £5 each, of which the owners of the Berehaven Mining Company got 34,000 shares and the Mining Company of Ireland got 26,000 shares. One Timothy O'Brien objected, since he did not want shares in the new company or to be liable for any charges in it, so on 9 November 1869 the company agreed to pay him £10,000 compensation.

Yet another new company, the Allihies Copper Mines, with a capital of £80,000, was incorporated on 11 November 1919. This still seems to have been in existence in 1922, for in July 1922 the Irregular Forces took two motor lorries and a quantity of motor accessories from the manager of the mines at Allihies, giving Mr. Ashe a receipt therefor. It must have closed soon after this, for its reopening in 1926 is recorded and its closure in 1931. In 1956 it was reopened by Can Erin, a subsidary company of the Canadian company Argussey. The place was drained out and modernized, but is at present dormant.

There is a local ballad:

The Old Berehaven Mine

Come all ye old Berehaven boys that toil both night and day,
I will sing for you a verse or two if you will attention pay,
Tis about this cruel mismanagement we had from time to time,
Which caused many a slave and others to leave the old Berehaven mine.
Twas opened by four Wicklow men, again you'll find I'm true,
And the old Berehaven boys of mining little knew,
And when it progressed rapidly with prospects fair indeed,
It was opened by the Puxleys and managed by John Reed.
We cannot praise the Puxleys, I'll tell you the reason why,
They caused us to eat the Indian meal & kept our wages low.
They spent their dimes in foreign climes on the choicest of high wines
And their orders were to starve us out in the old Berehaven mine.
It was in the year 1815 as I do chance to write
There was copper in this good old mine which at times was brought to light.
Then they sent Henry Pascoe, that reprobate of prime,
To become a second captain in the old Berehaven mine.
He longed to be promoted, he kept running to and fro,
At length he was made manager and John Reed was forced to go.
Oppressed by those cruel tyrants we could no longer stand,

119

We struck to oppose him and joined both heart and hand,
And when we used to walk about in abject poverty
Which caused many to roam far from their home across the deep blue
sea.
There is a rumour going about how this old mine was sold
Unto a foreign company for a vast amount of gold.
When Crean became the manager Keelogue he did lay low,
He invented new machinery and let the water flow.

Leaving Allihies northwest along the Eyeries road, a few hundred metres outside the village one comes to a T junction. Here the road to the left goes back to Ballydonegan Strand and the link road on which is the 'landing place of the children of Lir'. The road to the right goes to Eyeries and Kenmare, also to Castletownbere. Immediately on taking this road ruins of a mine will be seen. Probably the first thing to be noticed will be a wall on the mountain side of the road, remarkable for the attractive colours of the stones with which it is built. This is the Dooneen mine. On the right side of the road will be seen a cobbled floor, with the remains of substantial walls. This is probably where the ore was crushed and the copper washed. Behind this are the remains of a large reservoir. Southwest of here is the main mine shaft, where a large wheel would lower the skips, buckets or baskets to let down the miners and bring back the copper ore. This shaft has been filled in, as have two

Allihies copper mines

120

shafts on the seaward side of the road. The horizontal tunnels in this mine run out westward under the sea to the little Blue Islands in the bay. The tunnels are now collapsing which, in turn, has caused the high cliffs offshore to cave-in. There is tremendous scope for walks in all this area but it would be dangerous to attempt to enter these mine shafts.

Behind the reservoir, at the northern end, are two small ring forts, close to each other. They are much eroded and are not marked on the Ordinance Survey map. They are site 149 in the Berehaven list.

It is said there is still much copper in this area, but owing to the difficulty of the terrain — so much solid rock, the depth at which the ore lies, and lack of water power — it would not be economical to work it under present market conditions.

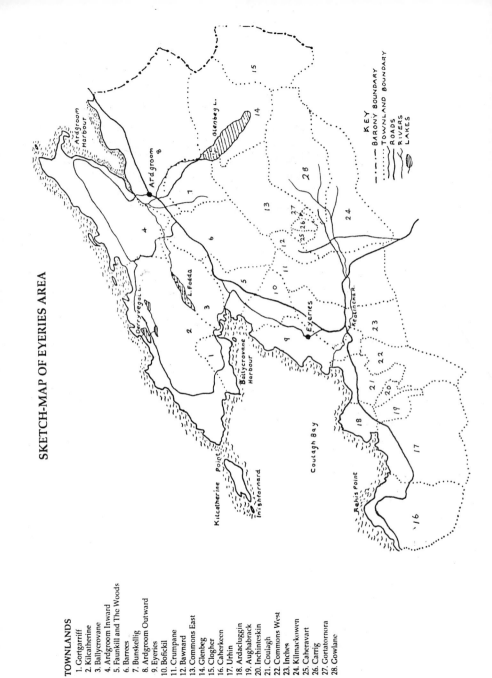

SKETCH-MAP OF EYERIES AREA

TOWNLANDS

1. Gortgarriff
2. Kilcatherine
3. Ballycrovane
4. Ardgroom Inward
5. Faunkill and The Woods
6. Barrees
7. Bunskellig
8. Ardgroom Outward
9. Eyeries
10. Bofickil
11. Crumpane
12. Bawnard
13. Commons East
14. Glenbeg
15. Clogher
16. Caherkeen
17. Urhin
18. Ardacluggin
19. Aughabrack
20. Inchinteskin
21. Coulagh
22. Commons West
23. Inches
24. Kilmackowen
25. Caheravart
26. Carrig
27. Gortatornora
28. Gowlane

KEY
—·—·— BARONY BOUNDARY
·········· TOWNLAND BOUNDARY
ROADS
RIVERS
LAKES

Chapter 13
Allihies to Eyeries

North of Dooneen is a little cove with a boat slip, a cave and a stony strand. This is Trawnferla, or the 'strand of the Pearl'. It is so named after a ship said to have been wrecked here many years ago: its treasure is said to be buried in a nearby field known as *Cúm an airgid*, but we are assured that the field has produced no sight nor sign of treasure!

In my researches I located some 30 vessels named Pearl, of whom one of the following would have been the most likely to have been wrecked at Trawnferla. There was a naval ship in the fleet against the Armada in 1588. A naval ship was stationed in Kinsale in 1695 and another in Bantry Bay in 1797. There was also a Pearl in the navy in 1667.[1] One of the vessels in George Anson's voyage around Cape Horn in 1740 was HMS *Pearl*, which found refuge in Brazil.[2] In 1757 a privateer was fitted out in Cork (150 ton, 18 men and 8 guns. Captain James Rea. Owners and setters out Paul Meyler & Company, Merchants, Cork).[3]

In the cove at Trawnferla have been found a couple of cannon balls, a lump of flint about the size of a man's head and some wreckage, the quality of which impressed the local seamen, one of whom said to me that it was beautifully dowled. Flint is not a native rock here and must have been brought in from outside; most likely it was ballast.

Beyond Trawnferla, after a sharp bend, will be seen a cave on the left side of the road: this is almost certainly a medieval mine. Further on there is a bungalow on the right and immediately after the next bend the road widens and there is a lane to the right and a field with a small stream on the left. Cross the stream here, continue on over the field and through a gap into the next field and turn right up by the wall and here will be found site 80 Reentrisk, which is not marked on the Ordnance Survey map. It is marked on a 16th-century map of Beare and Bantry in the Public Record Office, London. (See *JCHAS* vol. 63 No. 97, 1958). We are unaware of it being mentioned anywhere else, not even by Bishop Dive Downes in his very exhaustive visitation in 1699-1700, and it was this Public Record Office map which first drew it to our attention. Basically it is a ring fort, a very much ruined one, inside which is built an 8th- or 9th-century church. The door is on the southwest side of the church and its jambs lean towards each other. The window is at the southeastern end and is splayed. Within the church is a killeenagh and outside the northwestern end is what appears to be the remains of an entrance to a souterrain. The whole would appear to have been a monastic site. The headland to the southwest of the church is marked on the map as 'Pointnadrimna' but it is known locally as 'Pointnadisert', which would indicate a hermitage. In the southwest corner of the field adjoining the church is a group of stones, some of them recumbent, but others standing. They make no discernible pattern and are known locally as 'the cell'. The local name for this church is *teampall an díthreoigh*, but the fields around it are known as 'na diara'.

Marked on the Ordnance Survey six inch map, two fields southwest of this site, are 'Natural Arches', a chasm perhaps 30m deep with a natural bridge at each end. It is told locally that a ship was wrecked off the rock shore near here in a fog and the crew got safely ashore and climbed up the cliffs. The captain and mate were in front and they happened to reach one of the natural arches and got safely across. The crew were not so lucky and, unfortunately, in the fog picked the chasm instead of the arches and were all lost.

The lane opposite where we came in leads over the side of Knocnagallaun (incidentally, we have never succeeded in finding the gallaun!) down to Caherkeen, but the road takes one around the western side of the hill to the old Reentrisk school and through the Gap of Gortahig, from where it climbs above the cliffs to the hill over Caherkeen, with fine views all around. On this road, between it and the cliffs, will be seen two rough circular patches on the ground, one about 25m in diameter and partially surrounded by large stones, the other about half this size. They may indicate where forts once stood, but the present remains are too faint to be positive. The road runs through a low circular mound, which might also indicate a fort, and there also appear to be traces of prehistoric field sites. More positive evidence is that the place is known locally as 'Daingin' and there is rock close to the cliffs called 'Carrigdangin'. This is site 177 Caherkeen on the Berehaven list.

Near the top of the hill there is a gap in the mountains to the right and here on the cliff face is a cave, intriguingly known as 'the house of the lazy boy'. The only explanation I could get was 'he used to sit there and throw stones at passersby', and it does not look the kind of place where there would be many passersby!

From the highest point of the road here and the descent on the other side there is a fine view of the Kerry mountains and of the valley between here and the Slieve Miskish mountains.

In this valley, west of the Slieve Miskish mountains, are many archaeological sites, most of them much weathered or damaged. At the foot of the hill, by a grotto, the Eyeries road turns right and then left over Caherkeen Bridge. But if instead one continues straight on at the bottom of the hill one comes to two small, well-shaped standing stones. 60m apart and at right angles to a modern fence. This is site 86 Caherkeen, and is not marked on the Ordnance Survey map. It is difficult to decide what it is, but adjacent to it is a lane which is fenced with stone slabs and is very wet. It could supply quite a flow of water and the whole may be the remains of a much destroyed mill site. On the other hand it might well be a portal between the lands of two neighbouring clans, but then one would expect a line of boulders reaching out from each of the standing stones.

Continuing down this road brings one to Travaud Strand and a pier, where the road turns southeast to rejoin the road we have just left.

Cross over to the eastern end of Travaud Strand and, a few fields along the shore, will be found site 87 Urhan. It is not marked on the Ordnance Survey map and is a neatly shaped standing stone about 1m high.

Before leaving the Caherkeen area there are a few rather undistinguished sites which should be pointed out, if only to make some assessment of the population here in prehistoric times.

As one comes down the steep hill to Caherkeen, below the road on the south will be seen site 82, now little more than a circular patch of brighter coloured grass which clearly shows where there had once been a large fort. The diameter is 35m and this is the only measurement it is possible to take.

Site 81: near the end of the straight road running south from the grotto at Caherkeen is an avenue to a house on the left side of the road, and, in the righthand corner of the last field through which this avenue runs, the Ordnance Survey indicates a 'Killeenagh Burial gd.' It is said locally that it is a fort, and this would be consistent with the norm, but it is much too destroyed for positive identification. This site is one field in from Caherkeen Bridge, just around the next corner. Site 83 is a small standing stone, measuring .91m by .45m by .35m. Site 84: this is not marked on the Ordnance Survey map and must be considered a rather doubtful site. It is a roughly circular mound, part of which does appear to be artificial and there is a hole in the side which might be the entrance to a souterrain, but looks more like a badger's or fox's den, while boulders lying on top of the mound may be the remains of a ringwall. The local name for the place is 'the house under the ground', which would seem to indicate the presence of a souterrain.

Between sites 82 and 84, along the side of the mountain at an altitude of about 100m, are four small much eroded forts and, higher up at about 300m, is an overhanging rock making a small cave. A line of quartz runs along the roof of this cave and there are signs of burning, so it may be a prehistoric copper mine. These sites may be found by turning off the main road to the right, just before the straight road from Caherkeen grotto turns sharply left. About halfway up the road deteriorates into a bog road, but there is a turning place and opposite this, through a gate on the right, the above sites will be found.

A little further on, to the left of the road and near a clapper bridge over a small stream, will be found Site 85 Caherkeen, which consists of two low standing stones and one small stone, standing edgeways. Locally it is said to be 'the burial place of a woman who was murdered while milking a cow'. It was also said that the flagstones used to build the clapper bridge were taken off it, which seems very probable.

Two km northeast of Caherkeen is Urhan old school, now a shop and post office, and just before one rounds a corner to the building there is a narrow laneway to the left which bears right further on. The lane, especially in the lower part, is very wet. It is fenced with stone slabs set close together, which has the effect of retaining water in it rather than keeping it dry. The field into which the lane runs, or should I say flows, is a very marshy one but shows signs of having at some time been well-drained. Northwards of this lane is a megalithic monument consisting of a standing stone, two recumbent stones and a boulder dolmen.

About 100m northwest of the monument is a disused copper mine; its shaft is enclosed by a semi-circular bank of rubble. It is conceivable that the lane may have been a mill stream. The site is on the southwestern side of the bay at Travara Strand and neither the mine nor the megalith are marked on the Ordnance Survey six inch map. It is site 181 Urhan. The name of the mine is Coad (locally pronounced 'Co-Head'). North of this across the Kenmare River on Coad Mountain in Co. Kerry is another copper mine of the same name, which was worked in prehistoric times and also by Sir William Petty in the 17th century and again, for a short period, in 1808. It lies between Coad Mountain and Derrynane. There is a line of six standing stones between the mine and Derrynane Harbour which is believed to be a signpost between these two places, and there are other traces of megalithic remains here. It is highly likely that these two Coad mines were contemporaneous.

I am indebted to Mr Connie Murphy, N.T., who tells me he was informed that there was a railway line from the Urhan mine to the strand at Travaud. Mr Walter McGrath, of the *Cork Examiner*, whose interest had been aroused by the novel *Hungry Hill*, asked me to try and trace 'the truck railway that ran from Doonhaven to the mines each day', according to the novel. All I succeeded in finding was two railway tracks across the river at Pulleen, Dunboy. Then I recalled that, when driving down the old road, which this railway would have followed, across the main road near the old Urhan post office, I had noticed that there appeared to be a ridge across the road before each corner. The purpose for these ridges I couldn't visualize, but now it seems to me that the railway was a free running one, the trucks being allowed to coast down the hill from the mine, and these ridges were to slow them down to enable them to round the corners successfully.

If one is venturesome one could, with care, drive down this road but I would not advise anyone to try driving up it except one had a cross-country car! But there is another way of getting up to it and the mine. At Coad, we have, presumably, left our car parked at the Urhan post office. About 800m up the road northwest is Travara Bridge and the road to Travara Strand. Here there is a pleasant harbour, and strand and a small river, the latter requiring a little care as the pool at its mouth shelves deeply and steeply. But before we get to Travara Bridge, just after the new school on the left side of the road, a road branches right. Take this road for about 700m to a little ruined village on the bank of a small stream. Here the road divides right and left. Take the righthand branch and continue a few metres, stopping at the first gate on the left of the road. Inside this will be found site 168, which is a typical circular hut site. Its diameter varies from 4m to 4.50m, and the height of the interior is about 1m, the western side being sunk below the surrounding ground level, while on the eastern side the ground falls away outside the hut, and here the full height of the banked wall on the outside is 3m. The entrance, as usual, is to the southwest. There is also a small gap to the northeast but this is near the bank of the small stream and is almost certainly caused by erosion. The hut wall is about 1.50m thick and the site is on the south of the old road from Eyeries to Allihies.

In order to visit the old mines, continue up the road to the southwest about 1km to where, near a modern reservoir on the seaward side of the road, a road branches to the left and leads to the mines. The shafts are very deep and it is frighteningly impressive to hear how long it takes a stone to reach the bottom. Ahead of where we left the car the road dips sharply down to cross over the inevitable small stream and immediately rises just as sharply. Here a road to the right zigzags down the side of the hill and it is probably here that the truck railway ran down to the beach.

The road we have been on continues along the side of the hill over to Allihies and makes a splendid walk. The venturesome can follow the truck railway down to the lower road but the more advisable thing to do is to return to the ruined village where the road forked. Take the righthand fork and continue northeast for about 800m and one will come to the little village of Aughabrack, down in a hollow to the northwest of the road. Beyond this a road bears right and 800m or so up this road it joins another road where there is a gate and a sheep-dipping place. From here a very rough track leads southwards over the mountain and about 1.5 km up will be found the wedge grave at Coulaghard, which we have already seen in the distance from the other side of the mountain, at sites 73, 74 & 75, at Teernahillane. This is, as has been described before, an impressive megalith.

On returning to the car, go back to Travara Bridge and carry on northeast for about 1.5 km. One first comes to a house on the righthand side, then a shop; take the second road to the right. After 300m there is a gate into a large field on the left. From here will be seen, at the far end of the field, site 89 Coulagh, not marked on the Ordnance Survey map. It consists of three standing stones and three fallen ones, almost certainly the remains of a circle. A large quartz boulder lies at the base of one of the standing stones. Quartz, as the provider of copper, was regarded with respect by the prehistoric peoples and, as and when available, it is frequently incorporated into megalithic monuments.

Continue on this road until it joins another. This is the Aughabrack and Inchinteskin to Eyeries road, on which we have been already. Turn left here and continue northeast past a farmhouse and hayshed on the right. Stop at the top of the hill for a good general view of sites 94 and 90 Coulagh. In the field beside us, a little to the west, is a rather poorly built circular enclosure, and there are some stones that appear to have been placed in position artificially. The whole may be part of the monastic complex of the chapel of Coulagh, whose foundations may be traced in a field to the northeast below us here. This site can be more easily inspected from the Allihies-Eyeries road.

Also from here, to the north, will be seen the more extensive site 90, which can also be more conveniently inspected from the above mentioned road. The site consists of a scattered group of five standing stones spread over three fields, more or less parallel to a laneway leading down from the road to Pallas Strand. The largest stone stands just inside the fence to this laneway. It measures 2.90m by 1.90m by .80m. Along the top of this and down the northern side is a rough groove, which a Scottish antiquarian claimed was to allow the blood of the human sacrifice to flow off! As the stone is very rough and unshaped and one would need to be quite agile to perform the sacrificial act on its very pointed top, this is most unlikely. The next largest stone is in the same field. It also stands just inside the field fence, to the northeast of the largest stone, and its measurements are 1.55m by 1m by .80m. The other three stones are smaller and are in the field adjoining, to the west. These stones, strangely enough, are not marked on the Ordnance Survey six inch map.

From here to the west, about 1.5 km away, is site 88 Ardacluggin, a stone resting on a smaller stone, which may have been accidental but could just as easily have been intentional. It looks conspicuous on the skyline.

Travel back westwards for 100m or so along the Allihies road and stop at the first group of houses. Here a lane runs up south to the road we have just been on. To the northeast of this lane, in the second field, is a killeenagh. It is rather larger than usual and is also unusual in that there are the traces of two rectangular buildings standing at right angles to each other. This Coulagh Chapel. On the 16th-century map of Beara and Bantry in the Public Record Office, London, it appears as 'M'kolagh'. Bishop Dive Downes, during his visitation of 10-12 June 1700, mentions the ruins of a chapel at Coulagh, which he says is in Kilmannah parish.[4] Actually, it is now in Kilcatherine parish, but when the MacCartys of Clandermond owned the lands of Castletown, Inches, Dirrinny and Derrikeene, Killaconenagh parish extended to the shores of Coulagh Bay and Coulagh Chapel would have been in that parish then.

Three more sites are close together near here, Nos. 91,92 & 93 Eyeriesbegga, and could formerly be visited by going down the lane near the group of standing stones and continuing straight on instead of turning left down to Pallas Strand, but, since the collapse of the bridge at No. 91 in 1971, this is not now possible. All these sites, however, can be easily reached by going down the strand road from Eyeries, turning left and keeping straight on, instead of taking the right turn to the strand. The road ends a short distance down. Here, incidentally, was the house of Morty Oge O'Sullivan, and where he was shot in 1754. The flagstone of his house is said to have been just where the gate is now.

On 13 June 1738 an advertisement appeared in a Cork newspaper, *Tuckey's Cork Remembrancer,* to the effect that 'Murteach Oge O'Sullivan of Eyeries, in this county had been charged with harbouring Tories and Rapparees, and giving notice that he was prepared to stand his trial for the same said charge at the next General Assizes'. We next hear of him fighting in the War of the Austrian Succession on the side of Maria Theresa, who presented him with a richly mounted sword. In 1745 he fought at the battle of Fontenoy and in 1746 at Culloden, where, no doubt, he met John William O'Sullivan of Kenmare, the officer in whom Bonnie Prince Charlie placed most trust. Morty Oge was back in Eyeries at least twice before the fatal affray of 1754.

Site 91 is across the Kealincha River south of the site of Morty Oge O'Sullivan's house: a very graceful packhorse bridge known as Drehidagaddy (*Droichead na Gadaí*), 'the thief's bridge', which got its name in the following way.

Long ago when there were monks in the monastery of Coulagh, one very wild wet stormy night, much like the night in January 1971 when the bridge collapsed, one of the monks was in a most unhappy frame of mind and complained bitterly to the abbot of his lot in life; the cows had been troublesome, the milk had been spilt, he was soaked to the skin and frozen stiff and now he was late for supper. The abbot reproved him, saying he should thank God for the wet day as well as for the fine and ordered him to confess his sin. The penance the abbot imposed on him was that he was to stand under the bridge all night, up to his waist in water and with his staff in his hand, and, the abbot informed him, if by morning his staff had bloomed he would know his sin was forgiven!

So the poor monk stood there feeling more miserable than ever, when, above the storm, he heard somebody driving cattle. Thinking this a strange time to move them, he looked out and saw a notorious thief stealing the neighbour's cattle. The thief looked at the monk in astonishment and asked him what on earth he was doing there. The monk explained the position, whereupon the thief exclaimed: 'If that's the penance you get for a little thing like that, what on earth will happen to me? Move over quick and make room for me.' So they both stood there, in the water with their staffs in their hands, and when morning came it was the thief's staff that had bloomed and not the monk's. This bridge would have carried the old road from Eyeries to Allihies over the river.

Drehidagaddy, Eyeries (site 91)

Site 92 is in the second field northeast of the bridge. It is two well-shaped standing stones each about 2m high, set about 3m apart in the centre of a good grassy field. They are not marked on the Ordnance Survey map.

Site 93 Eyeriesbegga is a standing stone about 1m high, in the field

130

two fields north of the field containing site 92. It is not marked on the Ordnance Survey map. On our way down to the site of Morty Oge's house we passed the Shamrock guesthouse. Immediately behind this there used to be a holy well, Tobereenbanaha, but it is completely covered now. In the grounds of the same guesthouse, a few fields to the southwest between a path and a stream, is site 169 Eyeriesbegga. It is on the western side of the little stream that forms the boundary between Eyeriesbegga and Inches. The site consists of three standing stones in a line northeast-southwest. The two outside ones measure 1m by 1.60m by .50m and 1m by .70m by .50m and these stones appear to have been artificially, if rather roughly, shaped. The middle stone has fallen and is somewhat embedded, so it was not possible to take accurate measurements or see if it had been shaped, but it appears to be about the same size as the other two. About 10m south of these are two large

unshaped stones, one flat slab being so embedded in the ground it was not possible to take measurements of it. The other, which has fallen also, measures 1.50m by .90m by .50m. It is an unusual and rather puzzling site, but there is a similar site at Knocknacappul, Reenakilla, Lauragh (site 140).

Site 115 Eyeries: at the northern end of the village of Eyeries a road leads to the left, northwest, down to the sea. A short way down there is a shed on the left side of the road, with a gate and a stile beside it. Go in here and in the next field to the west, just inside a gap, will be found site 115, a small well-shaped standing stone, not marked on the Ordnance Survey map. The unusual feature here is that a figure has been pocked on the stone, something like a man in medieval robes.

Gallaun with inscribed figure, Eyeries (site 115)

Chapter 14

Kilcatherine to Ardgroom

The old school is situated a few hundred metres north out of Eyeries village, and just beyond it, on each side of the present road, will be seen traces of a medieval road, formerly the road to Castletownbere. A friend told me he remembered seeing a woman bringing up seaweed, in panniers on the back of a donkey, along this track.

A little further on is a small gap on the right, set back a little from the road. Here a path runs downhill beside a loose stone wall. It is quite easy to get through a gap at the bottom where a small stream flows. On the far side of this gap turn left and at the next fence will b e found site 126 Bofickil. This is a fine wedge grave, not marked on the Ordnance Survey map. The capstone has been removed as, owing to its proximity to the school, children used to play there and parents were afraid of it falling on top of them.

Continue on past the school for about 1.75 km to where the road is flat and there is a small wood on the left and on the right a gap through which a stream flows. Walk up this stream until the first field appears. In this will be found site 129 Faunkil and the Woods; this is an unusual site and looks like something that shouldn't be here at all! It consists of eight low standing stones set on edge to form a circle 2.30m in diameter with portal entrances at the northwest and southeast. It is on a low circular mound about 1m to 1.50m in height which rises somewhat higher behind the portal stones on the northwest, where it consists of earth, boulders, loose stones, rock outcrop and what may be small standing stones near the edge of the mound. One would say it is a miniature court cairn, but that is a type of monument not, so far, known in this part of the country.

Next turn, go left. The famous 4.7m ogham gallaun (see pp.73-4) stands out on the left. Pass the head of Ballycrovane Harbour. At the top of a slight rise is a road to the right, a cul-de-sac but good walking country. However, continue on to the next junction right. This is also a cul-de-sac, which leads down to Lough Fadda (the long lake), a place of peace and scenic splendour, and well worth visiting. The road along the coast dips down after this junction and then rises steeply. Before the final rise where a branch road on the right leads to the old Ballycrovane school (now a Belgian youth hostel), the road dips slightly.

Here, on the left overlooking Ballycrovane Harbour, is a boulder very famous in mythology, *An Cailleach Bhéara*. The Cailleach is featured in several poems, the best known of which is Padraig Pearse's 'Mise

Eire'. She was the wife of Manannán, god of the sea, who gave his name to the Isle of Man, and she waits here for her husband to return from the sea. Another reason given for her presence here is that one day St. Catherine was asleep outside the monastery of Coulagh, head resting on a Mass book. Along came the Cailleach Bhéara and ran away with the Mass book. St. Catherine gave chase. The Cailleach jumped from Coulagh to Eyeries Point and then onto Eyeries Island, from where she jumped to her present resting place at Gortgarriff. Here St. Catherine caught up with her and turned her into stone. At her first take-off she is reputed to have left her footprint in a rock at Coulagh and, just inside the fence from where we looked down on sites 90 and 94, this footprint is still pointed out.

In her own right the Cailleach was the goddess of the harvest,

An Cailleach Bhéara

which, no doubt, would account for her association — very slight, but none the less definite — with the festivals of Lughnasa, for Lugh was the god of the harvest. His festival was the last Sunday in July, Garland Sunday. On this day the people went into the mountains and up the hills to pick whorts (hurts, bilberries, blaeberries or fraochans), after which they held sports, with the emphasis on jumping.

The only connection the Cailleach Bhéara had with some of these festivals was that of three women. For instance, the festival at Drung,

133

Kilcatherine Church (site 117)

Carved stone head, Kilcatherine

Co. Kerry was opened by 'three nuns' and that at Cullen, near Millstreet, was founded by 'three sisters, Lasair, Inghean Bhuide and Latieran'. The Cailleach Bhéara was always associated with two other women, one of whom was always fair. T.C. Lethbridge associates the chalk figures of the Sussex Downs with the worship of the Cailleach which was common along the west coasts of Ireland and of Scotland. The Cailleach above Ballycrovane Harbour also overlooks three small fields, one of which is called 'the field of the fair woman'.

At some Lughnasa sites, such as Topped Mountain, Co. Fermanagh, the Duna, Portacloy, Co. Mayo, the Spellick near Ardavoyle, Co. Armagh and Keshcoran, Co. Sligo, there was a spot called the Cailleach's Chair. At Lough Crew in Co. Meath there is a fine cemetery of passage graves at Slieve na Calliagh; the cairns are traditionally reputed to have been dropped out of her apron by the Cailleach Bhéara. It is claimed she removed islands in Co. Kerry and in Scotland built mountains with stones carried there in her creel. Off the island of Jura, on the coast of Scotland, is a whirlpool called the 'Corryvreckin', which on an ebb tide makes a noise like an express train going through a tunnel. When this happens the local people say that the Cailleach Bhéara is washing her clothes, and when the snow lies on the mountains around they say that the Cailleach is bleaching her sheets.

As goddess of the harvest and wife of Lugh the Cailleach was known by the name Boi or Bui. The worship of Lugh was widespread throughout Europe and the city of Lyons in France is named after him.[1]

If we carry on along this road we soon come to site 117 Gortgarriff, marked on the Ordnance Survey six inch map as 'Kilcatherine Ch (in ruins) Stone Cross. Grave yd.' It appears in Taxation Rolls of Pope Nicholas III as 'Chellchatthigern' and of Pope Nicholas IV as 'Kylkaterryn'. In Bishop Dive Downes's 'Visitation of His Diocese' it is 'Kilcatierin'. Canon Lyons was of the opinion that this church was named after Kentigern, first bishop of Glasgow.[2] Brian O'Cuiv says it was a monastery of nuns founded by St. Caitiarin. Rev J.M. Cronin seems to confirm this when he says of Kilnamanagh that it was Kilmana, named after Ana, sister of St Caitiarn of Kilcatherine and niece of St. Senan. It may also be argued that Mungo, bishop of Glasgow, was not the only Kentigern and that it might mean 'a monk of Kent'. The only positive thing one can say about the name of the place is that one popular version, the Church of the Iron Cat, may be rejected out of hand.

The church is surrounded by a substantial ringwall enclosure. The arched entrance to the church is on the southern side and over it is a peculiar carved stone head, perhaps the 'iron cat' of imagination. It is rather sinister-looking, and friends who have seen similar heads in churches in Italy and Austria say it is pre-Christian and possibly connected with snake worship. In the graveyard there is an 8th- or 9th-century cross, of which there was a life-size photograph in the National Library.

The graveyard postulates a couple of problems. First there is a vault here and within it were a number of clay pipes. As an old custom was to smoke clay pipes at a funeral and break them on the coffin when it was being placed in the grave, this would indicate that a funeral had taken place here, but there is no sign of coffin or corpse. The second is a small, crude, undressed stone, on which a tiny cross has been inscribed, together with the inscription 'Mr Denison'. There was a Major John Denison in Colonel Phayre's Regiment of Foot in 1669 and I did have a note of an application to the commissar by a regimental officer for refund of the expenses of Mr Denison's funeral. However, I note that the memorial slab over the adjoining grave is to an O'Neill, so perhaps 'Mr Denison' should read 'Mr Denis O'Neill'. It is possible that the end of the name could have been weathered off, though it does not seem that there could ever have been enough to fit in 'eil'.

The following is an undated Mandate from Pope Eugenius IV (1431-1447):

To the Archdeacon of Ross, Mandate to collate and assign to Allan O'Hualloccayn, clerk of the diocese of Ross (who was lately dispensed by Papal authority as the son of an un-married man and an un-married woman related in the fourth degree of kindred) (1) to be promoted to all, even Holy Orders, and to hold a benefice even with cure and (2) having been tonsured, to receive and hold a canonry and the prebend of Kyllmana and Kyllcharrine [Kilcatherine] in Ross (provision of which was granted to him the perpetual vicarage of Kylldeochonynac) [Killaconenagh] in the said diocese, of the patronage of laymen and value not exceeding eight marks, void by the death of Gilbert Ohuolloccgyn, notwithstanding that the Pope recently granted him provision of the said canonry and prebend value not exceeding six marks. He is hereby specially dispensed on account of the said defect etc to receive and hold the said vicarage.

St Peters Rome 14 Cal. Dec.[3]

In 1432 Gilbert Ohuollocayn (O'Hoolahan) held the prebendaries of Kilnamanagh and Kilcatherine. He died before Ocotober 1432 and was succeeded by the above Allan O'Hualloccayn (O'Hoolahan). In 1591 Daniel O'Wollohan appears as rector and O'Linshigan as vicar. In a parliament held in Dublin in the 33rd year of the reign of Henry VIII (1542), it was ordained that Cormac FitzDonald was to be chief executor in the country of O'Sullyvan of the ordinances for the Reformation in Ireland.[4]

Continue down the road from Kilcatherine Church and pass a junction left (which, incidentally, leads to a raised beach where fossils may be found), then pass a house on the left. Ahead, to the left, is a group of houses down to which a road leads. Pass this and through a small gap with banks on each side of the road, immediately after which there is a crossroads. There are two ways one can get to site 118 Kilcatherine and this is one of them, so let's describe this one first and return here to what we will call Cross X for the second way. Here a shallow valley runs down to the sea at Kilcatherine Point and on each side of the valley a road runs down towards the sea. The one here at Cross X is the better one, so turn left here. The road soon turns right, past a sole house on the left, and then turns left down to the last house on this road, where commons lands begin. There is a turning place a little further on, but the road is grass-grown and may be slippy, so it might be as well to leave one's transport by this house and walk the rest of the way. From here will be seen, to the right and standing out in commons land, a large field with high stone walls. Go down to this field, which is about 200m away, and on the way down look out for site 119 Kilcatherine, which is close to the road on the righthand side. It is a circular hollow sunk into the ground to a depth of about 1.50m and inside it is a circular mound rising to almost outside ground level.

A very rough track runs along beside the nearest high wall up to the top of the hill. After passing this field one looks down on Kenmare River, and to the right below will be seen site 118 Kilcatherine. This is a good example of a wedge grave. It is set on a grassy mound in very marshy land, the mound being approximately 14m long tapering from 8m wide in the centre and again widening to 8m at the southern end where the grave is. The capstone of the grave is 2.50m long by 1.20m wide and rests on a stone measuring 1.45m to the west and at the northern end one measuring 1.30m long. At the east the grave has collapsed and the supporting stones broken.

But to return to Cross X. Here turn left (north) and continue on up the hill, where the road turns sharp left and comes out on commons land. Park here and walk in left, to the northwest and here will be found site 150 Kilcatherine, three standing stones. The first stands at an altitude of 100m and measures 1.20m by 1m and alongside it lies another stone, measuring 2m by .70m by .60m. Within sight of these, about 200m to the northwest, is another small standing stone measuring 1.30m by 1.15m. From this last stone can be seen, to the northwest in the valley below, the wedge grave, site 118. Also in the valley between these two

137

sites are traces of a causeway, so perhaps in the prehistoric period this was the 'official' route to the grave.

A couple of hundred metres further on along this coast road to Ardgroom one comes to a most noble slab of rock outcrop running downhill along the inner side of the road. At the foot of this hill a lane leads down to the sea, where there is a natural arch. A little further on the road comes to Derryvegal Lake, just before which a laneway runs in to the left and goes down to a rocky shore. About 800m northwest of here is Doonagh, an island attached to the mainland by a natural arch. The name Doonagh would imply a fort and it would seem a most suitable place for a promontory fort. Of it Thomas Johnson Westropp, in 'The Promontory Forts of Beare and Bantry', merely states: 'In Kilcatierin townland, near Derrycoosane, is a headland named Doonagh, evidently once fortified.'[5] He also published a plan of it. I have never been able to visit the place myself, but some experienced archaeological friends have and said they could find no evidence for a fort having been there. In 'The Archaeology of Berehaven' (O'Shea and Crowley, F.L.Y. Scheme, Kerry Diocese 1972), lack of time in which the project had to be completed and the inaccessibility of promontory forts forced their omission in this survey.

From Derryvegal Lake the road climbs until it reaches its highest point where a junction right leads back down to the main Ardgroom-Castletownbere road. But we will keep to the coast road. The view from here vies with the many fine views on this beautiful peninsula and some will feel it deserves pride of place. In a series of sweeping bends here the road drops rapidly towards the sea. Soon after the last bend a small road to the left goes down to Cleanderry Harbour.

Due north of here, along the coast, is a large wall standing in the middle of a field. This wall is site 158: it is about 12m high by 40m long and in its sides are stout square holes. This is the remains of a 'fish palace'.

Fish palaces were where the pilchards were cured, an industry that was important here in the 17th century. The pilchard was a small sea fish, similar to the herring but smaller and rounder. Fishing for them commenced on the first dark night in July. For the first three months they were large, fat and full of oil and owing to their dark colour were not popular on the export market, but still they were the most profitable of the six months fishing season, as they produced a large amount of oil for which there was a big demand. The fish palaces had very strong walls to keep out both heat and cold. The fish were packed in from the top and pressed down with weights and then the roof was thatched. In some cases they were smoked, in which case they were known as fumadoes, and in some places they were salted, but the pressing method seems to have been the most profitable.

The main countries the fish were exported to were Spain, Portugal and Italy. One man in Bantry, who had a fishery there from 1730 to 1745, is said to have made one shipment of 6,000 barrels. Bishop Pococke, writing in 1758, says, 'Pilchards they had about twenty years ago and forty years before that, so the common people have a notion that they will come twenty years hence, whenever they come their ruinous fish palaces will be re-built.'[6]

Ardgroom, Kilmakilloge and Dursey Island were important pilchard fisheries in the 17th century. Bishop Pococke also says the French came over to Sherkin Island for the pilchard fisheries and 'made great Fortunes out of them'.[7] They are also mentioned by other writers, such as Dive Downes and de Latocnaye. Sir William Petty opened his pilchard fisheries in Kilmakilloge in the year 1672. Thomas 4th Viscount Kenmare had fish palaces on his Bantry estate in 1769. Writing in 1810 Rev. Horatio Townsend has this to say of Bantry: 'In the beginning of the last century, the bay abounded in pilchards, the catching and curing of which gave, even at that time, wealth and employment to numbers, as many remaining vestiges of the houses employed for this purpose sufficiently attest.'[8] Before Charles Smith's time (1750) pilchards had deserted the bay but herrings and sprats remained in great profusion.[9] Pilchard fishing gave a great deal of employment and made fortunes for many, but it was very unpredictable: when it was good it was very good, but when it was bad it was very bad!

The fishing in Berehaven was always a profitable enterprise. The O'Sullivan Beare had an income of £50 from his lands and this went to the chief's wife as her pocket money, but he had between £500 and £600 from fishing dues and from the dues of vessels coming here for trade or protection. In a parliament held by Thomas Earl of Desmond in 1464 an act was passed for imposing a tax upon such strangers as came to fish upon the Irish coasts. In 1625 it was ordained that 'Fishing rights were to extend ten leagues into the sea, within which limits not any nation whatsoever shall fish without licence of the inhabitants.'[10]

When Queen Elizabeth I tried to acquire the fishing rights of Berehaven, Bantry and Baltimore she received the following sharp rejoinder:

1592 Declaration of the Commissioners for Ireland; they cannot find that the customs of fishing at Berehaven, Bantry and Baltimore belong to her majesty or were ever in her progenitor's hands. At the first conquest they were distributed amongst English gentlemen, the memory of whose names appear everywhere in the country, but at the time of Edward III & Henry IV the Irish prevailed and expelled many of them from their possessions. These Irish are now dutiful subjects, viz, septs of : MacCarthy More (Earl of Clancarre), Sir Owen MacCarthy's son MacCarthy Reagh, & the septs of the O'Sullivans who have showed themselves most dutiful and loyal subjects. If her majesty is entitled to any of these havens it will be found in the records of the Tower of London. No records here older than Henry VIII.[11]

Dr. A.J. Went says the pilchards were unpopular as food except with the Cornish miners at the Allihies copper mines, but the local people only valued them for the oil, which they used for lighting. In a very comprehensive article, 'Pilchards in the South of Ireland', he records the following:

Another tale is recorded by Tadhg Murphy of Waterville as follows — There is a strand west of Eyeries in the peninsula of Beare, called 'traig an tSeirdin' (the pilchard strand). A fisherman came from Scotland to the coast of Beare long ago looking for pilchards. He had a rig sailing vessel. He spent seven years one after another coming to Beare watching for pilchards but found none. He was lucky in the summer of the seventh year for the strand was packed with pilchards. He encircled them and filled his vessel with them but had to send for other vessels so plentiful were they. Then he hoisted sail and returned to Scotland a rich man after that night and was never seen around the coast again. The strand is still known by that name and always will be. All the old people tell that story.[12]

Leaving the turn to Cleanderry Harbour, down to which cars should not be taken, and continuing along the Ardgroom road one soon comes to another rockface beside the road. A road goes straight ahead uphill at the end of this cliff, but turn left here and about 700m will bring one to a sheltered harbour with a good pier. There is a reasonably good road down to this and room to turn. About one field from the harbour, to the northeast, is a cave, which runs straight out to the sea. It has two entrances at the landward end and it is possible, safe only on an incoming tide, to swim in to one and out through the other. The place is a very interesting geological fault.

A mile more on the road to Ardgroom brings one to the turn down to Pulleen, a pleasant place for swimming, walking or especially fishing off the rocks. The entrance to Ardgroom Harbour was described in 1887 as follows:

Ardgroom harbour on the south shore (of Kenmare river) although presenting a spacious land-locked area, with from four to six fathoms of water, has such an intricate entrance, over a rocky bar of 9 feet water only, that no vessel should attempt to

140

enter it. In sailing up Kenmare river the opening of Ardgroom will be very conspicuous. Knocknamona, its low dark-coloured western point, slopes down from an elevation of 208 feet, and is surrounded by outlying dangers. Kidney rocks, extending for more than a cable from its north side, are generally visible in the wash of the sea. One third of a mile N.W. by N. from the point is a rock, with 17 feet of water, rising suddenly from the deep water around, on which the sea breaks in heavy gales. Carrigavaniheen, 3 feet above high water, lies E by N $\frac{1}{2}$ N 4 cables from the point, and is comparatively clear of danger to the westward, but is foul to the eastward for one third of a mile.[13]

On the night of 22 December 1968, in a heavy gale, the fishing trawler *Seaflower* ran onto the abovementioned Carrigavaniheen Rock and was lost with all five hands.

The beach stretching across Ardgroom Harbour is what is known in geology as a 'tombola' and is formed by the stones and earth fallen from the nearby clay cliffs. At the outer end there is a pleasant sandy beach with a lot of sea shells. The tide comes right up to the base of the cliffs, so care should be taken to avoid being trapped.

About 500m further on we come to Pallas Harbour and Pallas pier, on the western side of Ardgroom Harbour. The 'palace' is in a field on the opposite side of the road to the sea. It is not so well preserved as that at Cleanderry. This is site 159 Pallas Harbour. In his correspondence Sir William Petty mentions a fish palace at Ardgroom belonging to Lord Anglesey and in 1673 and 1674 he is complaining of the poor return from his fishery at Kilmakilloge; he only got 40 barrels of oil in 1674 while his rival, Sir Francis Brewster, in Dingle Bay got 2,400 gallons in the same year. The 'Clerk of the Pallice' for Petty's fishery was Adam Goold.[14]

Friar O'Sullivan in his 'Ancient History of Kerry' records that in the 15th century there were 'Spanish colonies and factuaries at Cilemeculoge and Agroom.'[15]

Near Pallas pier there is a farmhouse at the foot of a hill on the seaward side of the road, behind which a lane leads up the hill. At the first gap on this laneway will be seen a killeenagh (marked on the Ordnance Survey six inch map as 'burial gd'). This is in the usual ringwall enclosure, but what is unusual is that in the burial ground there is a recumbent slab bearing the following well-cut memorial inscription: 'In memory of John Broderick, sailmaker, of Gosport, in the county of Hants, England, who died at sea on board the R.Y.S. Helen and was buried here August 21st 1869.' An elderly local man told me his father told him he remembered this inscribed stone and said it took three days to get it up to the burial ground. The yacht had come into Ardgroom in

141

search of a doctor but, failing to find one, the crew put to sea again. The sick man said that if he died he would like to be buried on this hillside and his wishes were duly carried out, the memorial slab being later sent over from England.

Chapter 15

Ardgroom to Glashananinnaun Stream

From Pallas pier to Ardgroom is approximately 2.25 km. About 1.75 km from Pallas the road turns left downhill and there is a farm entrance straight ahead on the corner. In here, southwest of the farm is site 131 Ardgroom Inward.

A search for the churches recorded on the 16th-century map of Beara and Bantry in the Public Record Office, London, led us to the finding of a place called 'Cummeendach' (the little glen of the tithes) on the northwestern side of Ardgroom Harbour, giving rise to a belief that one of the missing churches might be near here. Further enquires brought us to a field called *páirc-an-tséipéil* about 400m away, and in this field we found, almost completely covered by undergrowth, the remains of an oblong building. Local tradition says that it was used in the penal days, when only half the building was roofed and Mass was celebrated in the roofed end on wet days and at the unroofed end on fine days.

Between here and Ardgroom is Cappul Bridge, a good place for picnicking and exploring. Ardgroom is a pleasant village, picturesquely situated. Shortly before the year 1750 a Dr Lyne died here of smallpox aged 85. Apparently he was a believer in fresh air, for he would not allow any of the windows in his house to be glazed but always kept them open, and each window had another opposite to it. In his own bedroom were four, two open on each side of his bed. During the 50 years before his death nobody had died in the house, but after his death his son had all the windows glazed; within a few years several people had died there.

If one goes straight on up the village and instead of turning right for Castletownbere keep on by a wild-watered stream on the left, one will come after less than 2 km to Glenbeg, a deep, dark valley of most impressive aspect, and aspect is the correct word, for the scene here is constantly changing; the dark waters white-flecked on a windy day, in wet weather the many streams plunging down the sheer cliff face of the mountains. I have seen it in clear sunshine when all the country below was blanketed out in billowy fog, but the most surprising aspect was when the lake vanished, literally becoming invisible because of the reflections in it of the high encircling mountains. The best view point is from the Bun Skellig Hill, which rises steeply at the northwestern end of the lake and gives magnificent views all around, over the Kenmare River, the Kerry mountains, the lake below us and the mountains towering around it.

If one goes in to the head of the lake and walks back uphill to the northwest, one may come across a line of large boulders in which at one point, two large standing stones, possibly a portal and perhaps the whole may mark the boundary between two tribal areas. It is approximately where the boundary between Clan Laurence and Clan Dermot should be. Splendid country for walking this, and the fishing in the lake is good too.

A drive of about 1.5 km out of Ardgroom on the Kenmare road brings one to a farmhouse on the left; immediately after this a road runs down to the left, and soon turns right. Keep on until reaching a house on the right. Park here or at the gate before one gets to the house and climb up the steep hill opposite the house (northwest). Here will be found Dromard fort, so marked on the map, which is site 137 Ardgroom Outward (Dromard) on the list. It stands slightly to the north of Dromard Hill and is a very fine example of a triple ring earthen fort. Owing to the great amount of scrub in the fort and in a large portion of the fosse, we did not manage to do a complete survey of it. However, the banks are very high and the fosse extremely deep. In the fosse there is one good accessible entrance to a souterrain and another completely buried in bushes. In the fort there are at least three entrances to the souterrain, two of which a small person can go down.

Again from here one gets splendid views of the Kenmare River and the Kerry and the Caha mountains. Also, to the south can be seen sites 133, 134, and 136 at Canfea beneath Tooreennamna Mountain, an area rich in megaliths.

When we first visited this fort we found a dog had appointed himself as guardian of the place. After making his acquaintance he showed us a much shorter route to the fort than the one we had previously followed. Then, inside the fort he showed us two covered-up entrances to the souterrain that we had not noticed. We uncovered these and the dog went down one and came up the other. He then showed us an entrance in the fosse, additional to the good one we regularly used, but this was so heavily overgrown it did not prove possible to clear. The dog had a very poor opinion of me, as I was disinclined to go into the souterrain, and would catch me gently by the trouser leg and try to pull me in!

At the base of the fort, by the lane that forms the first ring of the fort, is a small stream with some stones standing in it, also a marshy place nearby. This could well have been the remains of a water mill.

On returning to the main road turn left and then, immediately, right, up a narrow road. Here there is a junction left which could be used to get to the Canfea sites, but it is a very bad road and turning is not easy, so I shall suggest another route later. Stop at the top of the first rise of ground and to the left of the road will be found site 136 Ardgroom Outward. This is marked on the Ordnance Survey six inch map as 'Lisnagat'. It is another earthen fort but has been largely reclaimed for agricultural purposes and little remains except the ring embankment. The entrance is said to have been halfway down the little hill we have just come up.

Before proceeding to Canfea and Barrakilly we will return to Eyeries to pick up some other sites on the main road.

Coming from Eyeries or Castletownbere, continue along the Kenmare road past the new Eyeries school and the playing field until you come to a disused farmhouse on the right before reaching the first bend on this straight section of road. Site 124 Inches will be found about two fields in from the road. It is a small ringwall enclosure, with the souterrain filled in. It is not of any particular interest.

A hundred metres or so further on, just around the first bend, a laneway runs in northeast from the right side of the road. At the end of this lane is a circular mound, site 125 Bofickil. The mound covers a chamber measuring approximately 3m by 2m by 1.50m. There are no traditions about it and it is believed locally to be of comparatively recent construction. Suggestions that it might have been a place for stowing ammunition during the Troubles or was a guardhouse for Bofickil Gap were satisfactorily disposed of by those who should know. The owners have always known it as 'the fowl house', but it seems rather substantial for such a purpose, yet the fact that there is nearby a very similar structure which is undoubtedly a cattle shelter may be evidence that its use was agricultural. However, recent study and reading on the subject has brought me around to the idea that it was a corn drying kiln.

Site 127 Bofickil: this site stands inside the fence on the seaward side of the road, on the second bend north of the gap. It is the remains of a large stone and earth embanked fort. It appears to have had a very deep fosse, signs of which are apparent on the north side but which has been completely eroded elsewhere. As foxes were using the souterrain for a den, the entrances were blocked up, but it is possible to see where they had been. Being on a sharp bend, it is an awkward place to park.

Continue on for about 1 km, past where a large section of the land has been removed on the right side of the road, and stop at the next house. Opposite there is a small gate. Go in through this and keep to the right, and a large flat slab of rock outcrop will be seen. There are a number of cuts on this and at the foot of the slab lies a large loose slab, very similar to the Faunkil and the Woods ogham stone but, before it broke in two, rather larger than the ogham stone. Locally it is said that this is where the Faunkil stone came from. Between here and the ogham stone below us is the very interesting site 129 Faunkil and the Woods.

Continue on downhill, pass the turn back to the coastal road and after passing over Barrees Bridge the road rises and then, on a corner, dips sharply. Here there is a track in to the left (west) through a marsh out of which rises a grassy hillock about 100m in from the road. On this hillock stands a smooth well-shaped square standing stone about 1m in height by .50m by .50m. Alongside is a recumbent stone, no doubt a fallen standing stone. This is site 130 Ballycrovane and is not marked on the Ordnance Survey map. Although it is only a short distance from the road, rubber boots are essential.

Continue on to Ardgroom about 2km away, but before leaving here it should be pointed out that two roads, one on the western side of Barrees Bridge and the other, a bog road, just opposite this site, lead southwards towards the mountains and give excellent scope for interesting walks.

At Ardgroom, instead of going down through the village, drive straight across up the road by the Holly Bar and on for about 1.5 km. Here, there is a bungalow on the right side of the road and beyond it is a junction right which will be recognized by its being quite wide and having substantial walls. Take this road. Approximately 200m in, the road dips down around a sharp bend to marshy land and here, a little to the west, will be seen site 180 Ardgroom Outward. This is a small well-shaped standing stone, not marked on the Ordnance Survey map. It is almost due north of site 132, about 400m away.

Across the road there is a gate where it is possible to turn a car. Park here and walk westwards for about 700m to find site 132 Ardgroom Outward. This site, not marked on the Ordnance Survey map, lies in marshy bogland at an altitude of 60m, near the base of Tooreennamna Mountain southeast of the village of Ardgroom. It consists of a standing stone about 1.50m high by 1m wide: at its base lies a large boulder of quartz. Next to the standing stone is a recumbent stone of similar size, probably a fallen standing stone, and a low circular mound of stones about 1m to 1.50m in height by about 3m in diameter. Mixed with these stones is a quantity of crushed quartz. Nearby to the north is a similar mound of loose stones, but on this there is no quartz. Further inspection of this site gives the impression that it was once enclosed by a large low ringwall and I am advised by a builder that the base of the mound is artificial.

Returning to where we left our transport outside the gate, we continue on eastwards out onto commons land, leaving stone-walled fields to our left and right. Towards the mountain, but quite close by will

146

Cairn, gallaun, fallen gallaun, Ardgroom (site 132)

Stone circle, Canfea, Ardgroom (site 134)

be seen site 133 Ardgroom Outward. This is the remains of a large cashel, or stone fort. It is in a very ruined condition but its diameter and circumference are plainly to be seen.

The next site is No. 134 Ardgroom Outward (Canfea), for once marked on the Ordnance Survey map, 'Stone Circle. Gallaun'. The circle consists of nine large standing stones, with an outlier, all standing on the perimeter of a large circular field. Whether the circular field and the circle of standing stones have any connection with each other is a debatable point, but there seem to be traces of a similar field on which sites 51 and 52 Kilmackowen would have stood on the perimeter. And further consideration of site 132 Ardgroom Outward makes one realize that the monuments here would have been on the perimeter of the low ringwall and not inside it. Two German archaeologists and two English ones referred to these as 'assembly places'.

Behind and to the south of the above stone circle is a mound 2m high, whose western side forms a gentle slope up which a narrow path runs. This path has on each side a kerb formed by shallow slabs of flat stones. Site 72 Clonglaskan has a similar mound but with no kerbs and it is obviously for rolling up the stones to get them standing by dropping them into holes. The mound at Canfea may have been for this purpose also, but it does not look as if it was; it faces in the wrong direction and why should it be kerbed?

About 200m northeast of site 134 is site 135 Ardgroom Outward, marked on the Ordnance Survey map as 'Caher'. This is an almost completely destroyed fort and little remains to be seen except the circular patch in the ground to indicate where it had been. One notable feature, though, is that on the perimeter of this patch stand four stones parallel to each other, almost certainly the entrance to the souterrain. On the edge of where the fort was, and rather overgrown, is a large boulder that is almost certainly a burial. A local man told me that this was the fort of the chief of all Beara and that he was buried in the field beside it, pointing out to me a slab of obvious rock outcrop! Between this site 135 and site 134 traces of a paved road have been found.

As has already been pointed out, these sites can be visited from Lisnagat, the fort at No. 135 above being about 800m from that at Lisnagat, but the land in-between is very marshy. A car could be taken up the road near Lisnagat for about 200m to where two rough roads meet and provide a possible turning place. It would then be advisable to walk southwestward along the rough road. Incidentally, Lisnagat has been translated as 'the fort of the cat', perhaps with the 'iron cat' of Kilcatherine in mind. It has also been suggested it is a corruption of 'Lisnagatri' (the fort of the copper workers), which seems a much more plausible explanation.

I have endeavoured to keep my account of megalithic sites to those that can be visited with comparative ease and it may be that the last two sites, those at Barrakilly, are the most difficult to find.

Leaving Ardgroom village by the Kenmare road, the second branch road to the left, or the third if one counts a newly made dirt road near the village, will take one to Dromard. This road is easily identified, as beside it is the first farmhouse on that side of the road. Continue on the Kenmare road past the turn back to Lisnagat and, after about 1 km, take the branch road to the right (southeast). This is another bad, narrow road with little room for turning or parking, so perhaps it may be advisable to park at the main road. Walk up about 800m, ignoring turns to the right, and take the first turn to the left. Go through the first gap and climb into the first field on the left. Here, on a mound covered with rich green grass, stand three most noble stones, site 164 Ardgroom Outward (Barrakilly).

The middle stone is a flat slab with a curved top. It measures 2.30m by 1.60m by .25m thick. The standing stones on each side of this measure 1.50m by .85m by .15m thick and 1.50m by 1.20m by .30m. There is a holly tree growing by each of these standing stones, the only trees in this field. It may be the remains of a circle of standing stones, but even in its present state it is a most beautiful and impressive picture. In the adjoining field to the northwest were found some kerbstones, possibly part of the old road that crossed the hill behind the woods of Lauragh down to Glenmore. Most of this road can be traced today. As so often happens, this splendid site is not marked on the Ordnance Survey map.

I first found these stones many years ago and then lost them and could not find them anywhere. I began to feel I was imagining things, though the friends who were staying when the site was first found assured me I was not but, on their next visit, when the search was resumed it proved equally unavailing. Then, in 1972, when the boys Denis O'Shea and Gerard Crowley were doing their survey of the megalithic sites of Beara, we were coming back after some fieldwork when one of the boys exclaimed: 'There's a standing stone!' We were late and I said I'd come out and look at it next day, which I did. It proved to be a roughly triangular-shaped stone set on edge by the side of an old track and just inside the southern fence of the Kenmare road, near Gorteen Bridge. It measured .80m by .90m by .40m. From is shape, size and position we took it to be merely part of the fence near it. However, when I looked up the slope on top of the stone, there, right in front of me, was site 164, the three great slabs missing for so many years! After that we deemed it worthy of a site number, 163 Ardgroom Outward

(Gorteen).

Returning from site 164, on reaching the main lane turn left instead of right and just at the foot of the hill almost 100m down is site 179 Ardgroom Outward (Barrakilly), which must be regarded as extremely doubtful and would require more expert examination. On a grassy low hillock there are a number of boulders, undoubtedly glacial erratics, though they do look as if they had been placed so as form, with patches of rock outcrop, a circle. Two of these stones are more than mere boulders, for they have been artificially shaped and placed in a standing position. Within this circle is what appears to be the remains of a semi-circle of stones, two of them placed in a standing position, around a low circular mound to which they may have been facing. On top of this mound a large flat boulder rests on three small boulders, almost certainly a boulder burial, though it lacked the pegstones that would confirm it as such.

Here we are on the western bank of the little Glashananinnaun stream and on the other side of this stream is a large area, Lauragh, Glenmore and Tuosist, very rich in megalitic monuments, but while we have recorded a lot of monuments in that area and it is tempting to include them, the Glashananinnaun is the boundary between the Barony of Beara in County Cork and the Barony of Glanerought in Kerry, and hence beyond our limits.

APPENDIX A

Reproduced by kind permission of the Cork Historical and Archaeological Society.
From the *Journal of the Cork Historical and Archaeological Society* vol. 75 no. 221 (1970).

A List of some Archaeological Sites on the Berehaven Peninsula

By D. Maddison O'Brien

In a paper read to the Royal Society of Antiquaries of Ireland on the 9th December 1919 (JRSAI, Vol. 51), Thomas Westropp said of the Berehaven Peninsula that the area called for long and systematic research for archaeological remains and folklore. The Great War broke out on the day in 1914 that Westropp was to begin work on Bantry and Beara and for four years leave could not be obtained to work there, and it would seem that such a survey has never been fully completed. Much as the writer would like to see this survey carried out, his much regretted lack of knowledge in the field of archaeology precludes the possibility of his undertaking the task himself. However, having, lived for ten years in the district and having during that time explored the area pretty thoroughly, he has a good knowledge of the local topography and it occurs to him that the following list of sites may be of interest, and perhaps encourage some more competent than he to undertake this very desirable survey. While the list does include all the sites of which the writer is at present aware, it is neither as comprehensive nor as systematic as he would wish, and he fears his unpractised eye may have caused him to overlook possible sites (or even, perhaps, to include some which are not in fact sites at all, but he has endeavoured to guard against this!). Also, a physical disability has prevented him from examining some sites on the higher mountains and has somewhat limited his explorations of the higher regions.

    For the sake of brevity standing stones have been grouped into the following classes: small standing stones of up to one metre in height; standing stones of between one and two metres in height; and large standing stones of over two metres high. The co-ordinates are for the Ordnance Survey Six Inch Maps and are from West and South. The map numbers refer to Co. Cork except Map No. 108 which is Co. Kerry.

1. DERRINCORRIN: hilltop cairn, approximately 11 metres in diameter, height 1.50 metres, elevation 598 feet, said locally to be "the grave of some big landlord or chief"! 34cms/2mms.

2. KEALAGOWLANE: Large Standing stone– 21.2cms/14.3cms.

3. KEALAGOWLANE: Large standing stone – 20.1cms/11.9cms.

4. CURRADUFF: Earthen fort, fort largely eroded. 9.3cms/10cms.

5. KILLENOUGH: Standing stone—9.9cms/1.9cms.

6. LEITRIM BEG: Large standing stone, with cross faintly inscribed thereon—1.9cms/5.2cms.

7. LEITRIM BEG: "Toberabanaha" Holy Well where a pattern was held up to within living memory. 1.9cms/14.9cms.

Map No. 103:

8. BALLYNAHOWN: Wedge grave, marked on map as "cromlech." 89.3cms/10.3cms.

9. LEITRIM MORE: "Gallaun"—small standing stone— 88.5cms/4.1cms.

10. LEITRIM MORE: Doubtful site not marked on map. Two small standing stones and one slab placed, apparently artificially, on a low mound amongst rock outcrop by a small stream.

11. CROOHA EAST: Large fort with well-defined fosse, but souterrain has been filled up— 82cms/.8cms.

12. CROOHA EAST: Circular mound, without ramparts and with only faint traces of a fosse, close by above

and known locally as "Lisbeg."—
82cms/2cms.

13. KILDROMALIVE: Marked on map as "caher" but seems much too small to be such and may possible be a large hut site or sheep enclosure— 69.5cms/4.8cms.

14. KILDROMALIVE: "Gallaun" large standing stone. 72cms/8.5cms.

15. CAPPALEIGH NORTH: "Gallaun," small standing stone. A cup-marked boulder lying on the edge of the road cutting nearby and a roughly circular patch in the field might indicate the site of an almost completely destroyed stone circle but the evidence for this seems insufficient. 69cms/.5cms.

16. DROMGARVAN: "Gallaun," large standing stone. 63.00cms/8.00cms.

17. KILCASKAN: Kilcaskan church (in ruins)— 64.50cms/14.00cms.

18. KILCASKAN: Monumental pillar—Ogham? stone, in graveyard at southeast corner of above.

19. KILCASKAN: Toberatemple—a well, in a hole similar to a bullaun, on rock outcrop upon which .has been cut a rude cross. A line of boulders, which may or may not be natural, curves down from the well to a nearby stream. (Behind the hedge on the opposite side of the road to the above). 65.50cms/14.20cms.

20. INCHINTAGLIN: "Cromlech"—52.50cms/5.50cms.

21. ADRIGOLE: "Cromlech"—52.50cms/4.50cms.
   The above, Nos. 20 and 21, have not been examined by the writer but from the terrain he is of the opinion that they are more likely to be glacial erratics

rather than any form of megalithic monuments.

Map No. 116

22. CROOHA WEST :	Cross inscribed on rock outcrop—73.3cms/60.3cms.
23. do. : do.	—74.0cms/57.3cms.
24. DRUMLAVE:	Gallauns—three standing stones in a row—70.0cms/59.9cms. Nearby is a medieval house site and possible pre-historic hut site.
24a.DRUMLAVE:	"Stone Circle," consists of about five stones standing edge to edge and looks very small to be a "circle." 69.0cms/58.9cms.
25. DRUMLAVE:	Earthen fort—66.0cms/48.9cms.
26. CROOHA WEST:	Much eroded fort, through which a modern fence runs. 74.0cms/60.0cms.
27. CROOHA WEST:	Earthen fort—65.7cms/53.3cms.
28. CAPPALEIGHNORTH:	"Gallauns. Cromlech"—boulder dolmen and two standing stones in a circular field—63.5cms/57cms.
29. CAPPANAPARKAEAST:	"Gallaun"—small standing stone, standing prominently on a hill—46.5cms/57.0cms.
30. DERREEN UPPER:	"Cromlech"—large boulder resting on three small stones on rock outcrop; looks to the writer more like a glacial erratic than a megalithic monument—34.1cms/56.1cms.
31. COOMGIRA:	"Gallaun"—large standing stone (3 x 2 metres)—30.8cms/49.0cms.

32. BOHER: Two small standing stones eight feet apart. Not marked

on map—7.5cms/31.3cms.

33. BANK HARBOUR: Site of Jacques Fontaine's farming and
                      fishing settlement 1700/1708 (JCHAS IV).
                      Although the walls of Fontaine's fort were
                      standing up to about fifty years ago there is
                      now no trace of them.—10.5cms/24.7cms.

34. LYRE: "Gallaun" standing stone—2.7cms/33cms.

35. LYRE: "Gallaun" standing stone—1.0cm/32.9cms.

                      The above two (Nos. 34 & 35) are very similarly shaped
                      and would appear to have been artificially
                      worked.

DARRIHEENDERMOT: 22cms/34cms. There are several references
                      to the Darriheendermot pillar stone (e.g.
                      JRSAI No. 50 pl. 52) but, while this area is
                      easily located, frequent searches by the
                      writer have failed to reveal any megalithic
                      monuments there.

Map No. 115

36. THORNHILL: "Childrens Burial Ground." Unusually for a
                      killeenagh, there is a well-cut headstone
                      here inscribed "Honora O'Sullivan Died 9th
                      July 1815 aged 3 months." 87.0cms/23.2cms.

CURRADUFF,
Rossmacowen: "Gallauns"—while the site has not been
                      inspected by the writer he is informed that
                      these have been removed by the landowner.

37. ROSSMACOWEN
COMMONS:Not marked on map—a natural cave, known as "tigh fá
                      thalamh," some twenty feet up a cliff face,
                      which may have been used as a human
                      inhabitation, perhaps as a penal days
                      priest's hide-out as there is a rock, roughly
                      the size and shape of an altar, known as

155

"the mass rock" nearby. 86.0cms/41cms (approximately) Elevation abt. 400ft.

38. ROSSMACOWEN
COMMONS:
Not marked on map—two large standing stones in rough ground—possibly an outlier and remnant of a destroyed circle. Nearby, to the southwest, is a small well built field, known locally as the "lios," in which there is a small standing stone. 80cms/35.5cms.

39. CAPPAGHAVUCKEE:
Not marked on map—boulder dolmen, the capstone of which is a flat slab, with some doubtful cupmarks, mounted on three small boulders. Nearby is a small standing stone. Both are on the edge of an old, now disused, road. 76.0cms/28.8cms Elev. 200ft.

40. RODEEN:
"Burial Gd. (disused)", probably a killeenagh. There is a standing stone in it.—50.0cms/19cms.

41. RODEEN:
Not marked on map. Standing Stone. 45.5cms/26.3cms.

42. RODEEN:
Not marked on map. Small standing stone 46.0cms/23.0cms.

43. RODEEN:
Not marked on map—an improbáble site, three small rough stones set on end in a line 3.0m and 1.3m apart, opposite which are two other similar stones, 3.5m apart and 4.70m and 7.20m from the others, probably remnants of an ancient road fence or that of a small enclosure. 45.5cms/28cms.

44. DERRYMIHAN WEST:
Not marked on map—four boulder dolmens, one of which appears to have collapsed, described in JCHAS, XXXIII, p. 66 as a "triple clochtaogle," but there is a fourth built into the boundary fence on the western side of the field. 38.0cms/21.5cms.

45. DERRYMIHAN WEST: Not marked on map—large standing stone, built into boundary fence. It seems probable that it was more than a single standing stone but in its present state it is not possible to say with any certainty. 37.5cms/21.3cms.

46. CLOONTREEM: Not marked on map—very good circular house site, in marshy ground but very dry inside even after very wet weather. Interior diameter 4.80 metres. 35cms/35cms.

47. FOILDARRIG: "Gallauns"—one large standing stone leaning southwards and two fallen stones of similar size. 28cms/23cms.

48. FOILDARRIG: Not marked on map—boulder dolmen— 26.5cms/30.5cms.

49. FOILDARRIG: "Holy Well"– a low circular mound in the centre of which are two holes .9 metres apart. They measure .8 x .4 metres and .6 x .4 metres and the rims are edged with loose stones. There is no sign of water in them. 23.5cms/32.6cms.

50. FOILDARRIG: Not marked on map—doubtful site, a circular mound possibly a hut site— 22cms/38.5cms.

51. KILMACKOWEN: "Gallaun"—large standing stone leaning to the west. 26.5cms/49.5cms.

52. KILMACKOWEN: Not marked on map. Small wedge grave, with finely cup-marked stone inside. In adjoined field s/e of No. 51—27cms/48cms.

53. KILMACKOWEN: "Gallaun"—large standing stone. 25.5cms/ 57.2cms.

54. CRUMPANE: "Gallaun"—standing stone –8.5cms/59.3cms.

55. INCHES: Not marked on map. Two small standing stones about a metre apart on the bank of a stream which washes the base of the larger, exposing the pegging which keeps the stone in place. 1cm/48.5cms.

56. FOILDARRIG: "Killeenagh. Burial Gd. (Disused)." The writer has failed to find this but there is a lot of stones at one end of the field so the site may have been cleared—30cms/24.5cms

57. FOILDARRIG: "Burial Gd" very much overgrown and difficult to examine 27.3cms/23cms.

58. DROM NORTH: "Killeenagh Burial Gd. (infants)." 21.5cms/10.5cms. Very small, much overgrown.

59. DERREENATAGGART
MIDDLE: Not marked on map. Large thin standing stone. 21.8cms/13.2cms.

60. do.:   Not marked on map. Large thin standing stone, southwest of above—20.0cms/13cms.

61. DROM NORTH: Not marked on map. Southwest of the above are two gate posts, one of which is firmly set and could well be a standing stone : very similar in shape to Nos. 59 & 60.—16.5 cms/11.5cms.

62. DROM NORTH: Not marked on map. Collapsed standing stone. 15.0cms/6.7cms.

63. DROM NORTH: Not marked on map. Well-shaped small standing stone. 18cms/7.3cms.

64. DROM SOUTH: Not marked on map. A small well-shaped stone similar to the above, standing in the boundary fence between Drom North and Drom South, which could be a "standing stone"—19cms/7.5cms.

65. CURRADONOHOE: "Killaconenagh Church (in ruins) Graveyard (disused)" (JCHAS, XXIX p. 35 & IIIA p. 112). Graveyard contains some interesting headstones but is now very much overgrown and impenetrable. 12cms/11cms.

66. DERREENATAGGART
WEST: "Gallauns"—Circle of nine standing stones, two of which have collapsed. The owner of the land informed the writer that he was told by his father and grandfather not to plough the land to the west of this circle as "there was a layer of burnt stones under the ground." 13cms/19cms.

67. DERREENATAGGART
WEST: Not marked on map—stone-lined trough set into side of low mounds—(Fulacht Fiadh) 14cms/19.5cms.

68. FANAHY: Not marked on map. Five bullauns in rock outcrop. 5.8cms/4.5cms.

Map No. 114

69. FANAHY
(Knockavaud):   "Gallauns"—one large standing stone and two recumbent ones, one of which fell in 1969. The one which was already fallen has cup-marks on it as also has a section of rock outcrop or covered boulder in the same field. 92.1cms/5.2cms.

70. FANAHY: Not marked on map. Circular hut site— 91.5cms/8.5cms.

71. FANAHY: Not marked on map. In adjoining field north of the above site (No. 70)— Indefinitive site; a group of three or four small standing stones apparently forming no pattern and another one, well-shaped, a

short distance away in the same field. 91.3cms/9.3cms.

72. CLONGLASKAN: "Gallauns"—near main road west of stream by Cahergarriff School, a very interesting site—semi-circular group of six standing stones (three of them being large) in the arc of which is a boulder dolmen around which are about five small stones set on edge. Nearby is a large square boulder, the whole site being enclosed by a shallow circular depression in the ground. 87.0cms/2.0cms.

73. TEERNAHILLANE: Circular mound, probably a platform fort 84.0cms/16.3cms.

74. TEERNAHILLANE: Similar mound to the above but very much damaged— 85.5cms/16cms.

75. TEERNAHILLANE: Boulder dolmen, against which rests a cup-marked slab, alongside which are two standing stones and a recumbent boulder— 81.3cms/14.3cms.

76. KNOCKROE WEST: "Toberabanaha"—not inspected by the writer. 55.2cms/0.5cms

77. KEALOGE: "Gallaun", Small standing stone— 44cms/0.5cms.

78. ALLIHIES: "Kilnamanagh Church (in ruins)"— 29.8cms/4.0cms.

79. ALLIHIES: Dooneen—22cms/13.5cms. Promontory fort mentioned by Westropp (JRSAI. Vol. 51) but the writer has so far been unable to trace this. However, he has not yet had the opportunity to follow up Westropp's list of promontory forts in this area.

80. REENTRUSK: Not marked on map—A killeenagh inside the ruins of an early church which is

surrounded by a circular enclosure. The local name for this is "teampall na direoige" and the fields around it are called "na diara." The point of land stretching into the sea near this site which is marked on the map as "Pointnadrimna" is known locally as "Pointnadishert." The older people say a pattern used to be held here, but apart from this, there seems to be no local tradition concerning the place. In the sixteenth century map of Bantry and Beare in the Public Record Office, London No. MPF. 194, (JCHAS, LXII, No. 197) this church is shown but it is not mentioned by Bishop Dive Downes in his tour of the area in 1700. 13.5cms/20.2cms.

In the adjoining field to the south/west is an indeterminate group of stones known locally as "the cell"—13.2cms/19.5cms. The writer is indebted to Master Denis O'Shea, Caherkeem, Eyeries, for bringing this site, and several others in the Caherkeen area, to his attention.

81. CAHERKEEN: "Killeenagh Burial Gd." said locally to be a fort but is much damaged and difficult to interpret. 42.5cms/36.5cms.

82. CAHERKEEN: Not marked on map—well-defined site of a large fort now destroyed— 35.5cms/35.6cms.

83. CAHERKEEN: Not marked on map—small standing stone —37.5cms/32cms.

84. CAHERKEEN: Not marked on map—a doubtful site consisting of a rough circular mound with a hole in the side which could be merely a foxes' or badger's den but is known locally as "the house under the ground." Perhaps a much destroyed fort—34cms/26cms.

85. CAHERKEEN: Not marked on map—two standing stones and one small stone set on edge, said locally to be the "burial place of a woman who was murdered while milking a cow" and the writer was also told that some stones have been removed to make a bridge so perhaps it may have been a hut site. 38.5cms/26.0cms.

86. CAHERKEEN: Not marked on map. Two small standing stones about .6 metres apart, one in a modern fence but at right angles to it, probably merely remains of an ancient fence. 42.5cms/39.5cms.

87. URHIN: Not marked on map. Small standing stone, well shaped. 50.5cms/39.5cms.

88. ARDACLUGGIN: Not marked on map. Doubtful site, large standing stone which leans onto a smaller one—64.5cms/50.5cms.

89. COULAGH: Not marked on map. Three standing stones and three fallen ones, probably remains of a circle. 73.5cms/46cms.

90. COULAGH: Not marked on map. Small standing stone—75cms/49.5cms.
Small standing stone—76cms/49.3cms.
Small standing stone—76.5cms/49.4cms.
Large standing stone—77.5cms/49.4cms.
Standing Stone—77.7cms/50cms.

91. EYERIESBEGGA: "Drehidagaddy Bridge"—(The Thief's Bridge). Medieval packhorse bridge—83.3cms/54.5cms.

92. EYERIESBEGGA: Not marked on map. Two well-shaped standing stones, three metres apart—84cms/55cms.

93. EYERIES Td: Not marked on map. Standing stone—83.7cms/56.6cms.

94. COULAGH:

Map No. 128

Not marked on map. Killeenagh, site of Coulagh church, now completely vanished but mentioned by Bishop Dive Downes (as "M'Kolagh") in the year 1700. 75.3cms/48.0cms.

95. DUNBOY:

"Dunboy Castle," ruined mansion of the Puxley family. 12.5cms/58cms. "Castle (in ruins)" – O'Sullivan Beare Castle destroyed in 1602. 15.5cms/58cms.

Map No. 127

96. GOUR:

"Gallaun"—standing stone said to have the ogmic inscription "cari" (JRSAI No. 50p. 152) but the writer has been unable to find this inscription 72.5cms/59.3cms.

97. KNOCKROE WEST:

"Gallaun"—large standing stone which fell about 1967, a fine specimen— 43.5cms/31.6cms.

98. KNOCKROE EAST:

"Caheraphuca"—ring fort, much damaged. 48.5cms/40.5cms.

99. KNOCKROE EAST :

Not marked on map, a somewhat doubtful site. Large standing stone which has fallen onto a smaller one, both in a field fence— 47.5cms/38cms.

100.KEALOGE:

"Gallauns"—two standing stones standing at right angles to each other, 3.5 metres apart. 50.3cms/60cms.

101.KILLOUGH EAST:

Not marked on map—good example of wedge grave, with possible cupmarks on capstone—14.5cms/38cms.

102.KNOCKROE WEST:

Small ring fort, of no special interest— 41cms/36cms.

103.KNOCKROE WEST: Ring fort—40.5cms/36cms.

104.KILLKINIKIN EAST: Ring fort—36.3cms/34.3cms.

105.KILLKINIKIN EAST: Ring fort—31.2cms/36.8cms.

106.KILLKINIKIN WEST: Ring fort—24.3cms/32cms.

107.LOUGHANEBEG: Ring wall enclosing large circular partially stone-faced mound, the fosse between being some two metres deep towards the west. To the east the ringwall has vanished and the mound and fosse eroded. It is interesting in being much lower and flatter than other forts in this area. 40.7cms/29cms.

108.LICKBARRAHANE: "Gallaun"—While it is possible that a fallen "standing stone" may be hidden in the long sedgy grass in this vicinity, all the writer has been able to find are two small standing stones, .5 metre apart, which he believes to be merely the remains of a boundary fence. 47.5cms/30.7cms.

109.BRACKLOON: Not marked on map—rockcut souterrain which was written up by the late Professor O'Ríordáin. 61.5cms/32cms.

110.KILLOUGH WEST: "Killeenagh Burial Gd. (Disused)." Has not been seen by the writer—13.3cms/31.5cms.

111.BALLYDONEGAN: "Killeenagh Burial Gd. (Disused)." Has not been seen by the writer—24.7cms/55.5cms.

112.CANALOUGH: "Signal tower (in ruins)." 33cms/13.1cms.

Map No. 126

113.LOUGHANE MORE : Fort—81.8cms/25.3cms.

114.BALLYNACARRIGA: Not marked on map. Three large boulders resting on smaller stones, possibly boulder dolmens. One is in the field to the northwest of the road, a second built into the fence beside it and the third in the field on the opposite side of the road, in which field there is also a rough low circular mound. 64cms/32cms.

Map No. 101

115.EYERIES:

Not marked on map. Small standing stone 86cms/3.3cms.

116. GORTGARRIFF:

Not marked on map; more of mythological rather than archaeological interest; a rock known as the "Cailleach Béara" well known in Irish legend. 85.5cms/23.5cms.

117. GORTGARRIFF:

"Kilcatherine Ch. (in ruins) Stone Cross. Graveyard" (JCHAS, IIIA & XXXIX). The entire site is surrounded by a ring wall and over the church door is an interesting carved head. 80cms/26.7cms.

118. KILCATHERINE :

Not marked on map, a wedge grave on a mound on a mound in marshy ground. Nearby are similar mounds/ 68cms/33cms.

119. KILCATHERINE:

Not marked on map, a very doubtful site consisting of a circular hollow with a mound inside, the purpose of which it is difficult to determine. 66cms/28.8cms.

Map No. 102

120. CAHERAVART:

"Stone Cross Killeenagh Burial Gd." Large ring wall enclosing an area of approximately 200 metres in diameter in which there is a stone-faced mound on top of which are the killeenagh and a rude cross, also a sunken pile of stones which may possibly be a collapsed beehive church. Within the enclosure are also signs of several house sites. 22cms/2cms.

121. CAHERAVART: "Gallaun"—standing stone, adjoining the above site. 20.7cms/1.8cms.

122. CRUMPANE: Not marked on map. Standing Stone—10cms/.5cms.

123. CRUMPANE: Not marked on map. Remains of a much eroded fort. About three hundred metres up the mountain to the north of this is a rockface which is said locally to have been a prehistoric copper mine and to the writer's unpractised eye it looks as if this may well be so. He has also been told that there are five more forts in the immediate vicinity of this one, but he has not seen these and has not yet had the opportunity of looking for them. This is a difficult area to give accurate co-ordinates for but the fort is approximately 13.5cms/6.5cms.

124. INCHES: Not marked on map. A small fort said to have had a souterrain which is now filled in. 3cms/2cms.

125. BOFICKIL: Not marked on map. A circular mound under which is a stone-lined chamber approximately three metres by two by one and a half. This is said locally to be of fairly recent construction and it must be regarded as a doubtful site until expert examination is made. 7.5cms/5.7cms.

126. BOFICKIL: Not marked on map—wedge grave, the cap and end stones of which have collapsed—2cms/9cms.
On Knockeen hill to the northeast of this site is a large boulder resting end upwards on rock outcrop, but while this is conspicuous and from a distance looks like a standing stone and even appears as if it may have been artifically placed, yet, the writer feels, it must be regarded as a glacial erratic—or,

perhaps, the trigonometrical station marked on the map there! 3.5cms/11.7cms.

127. BOFICKIL: Large stone walled fort, much damaged and the souterrain of which has been filled in. 7cms/14cms.

128. FAUNKIL and
THE WOODS: "Gallaun"—Large standing stone bearing the ogmic inscription "Maqi Decceddas Avi Turanias." A rock ledge just below the Castletownbere/Kenmare road (10.5cms/ 22.5cms) north east of this site is pointed out by local people as the spot from which this standing stone was cut. 4cms/20.6cms.

129. FAUNKIL and
THE WOODS: Not marked on the map, an indeterminate but very interesting site—a circle, 2.3 metres in diameter, of very low standing stones, eight in number, standing on the end of a low mound about 1/1.5 metres in height. Behind the two portal stones on the north west of the circle the mound rises a little higher on which are some boulders. loose stones and rock outcrop. 5cms/17.7cms.

130. BALLYCROVANE: Not marked on map—standing stone on grassy mound in bogland. The stone is well shaped and on the ground beside it is a recumbent stone measuring 2.20m x .60m x .30 metre which may be a fallen standing stone—18cms/31.5cms.

131. ARDGROOM
INWARD: Not marked on map: a field known as "parc an tséipéil" in which there is the remains of a building, probably those of one of the missing churches marked on the Dunlop map of Bantry and Beare (No. MPF. 194) in the Public Record Office, London (JCHAS, LXIII).

132. ARDGROOM
OUTWARD: Not marked on map—standing stone at the foot of which lies a small boulder of quartz, and about 1.5 metres off are a large recumbent stone, probably a fallen standing stone, and a circular low mound of loose stones on which there is a good deal of crushed quartz. Nearby is a similar, but less high and less well defined mound of stones, with no quartz.—45cms/39cms.

133. ARDGROOM
OUTWARD: Not marked on map—very much ruined cashel. 51.5cms/42.5cms.

134. ARDGROOM
OUTWARD Canfea : "Stone Circle" "Gallaun." Circle of eight standing stones, with an outlier, on the perimeter of a large, almost circular field. Immediately behind the circle is a mound about two metres high with traces of a paved map leading up it, but this may be merely the base of a turf clamp. An interesting site. 53cms/44cms.

135. ARDGROOM
OUTWARD Canfea: "Caher"—almost completely destroyed fort, on the perimeter of which are four portal stones which may have been the entrance to the souterrain. 56cms/45.2cms.

136.ARDGROOM
OUTWARD: "Lisnagat"—very much overgrown fort, said locally to have a souterrain, the entrance to which is under the road running alongside the fort—51cms/48.5cms.

137. ARDGROOM
OUTWARD Dromard: "Dromard Fort"—a fine example, with very high banks, a deep fosse and a souterrain. Having a claustrophobic nature the writer has never ventured into the souterrain but

he is informed by those who have that there are three small chambers under the mound with two exits inside the fort, and on two occasions friends of his have entered through the souterrain entrance in the fosse and emerged through one of those inside the fort. Unfortunately, the entrance to the souterrain has now been filled up, because of sheep getting caught in there, and the interior of the fort has become very much overgrown. 50.5cms/ 54.5cms.

Map No. 108 (Co. Kerry)

138. CASHELKEELTY: "Gallauns"—Group of three standing stones, one a large one—57.8cms/20.9cms.

139. CASHELKEELTY: "Gallauns"—three standing stones in a row, besides which are three low stones set on edge, two at right angles to the third. 58.5cms/21cms.

Probably the stones known as 'Froude's Seat' (*Glanerought and the Petty-Fitzmaurices*) where Froude wrote much of his *History of the English in Ireland*.

The above two sites are beside an early, now disused, road, probably medieval.

140. REENAKILLA
Knocknacappul: "Gallauns"—On Knocknacuppal island in woodland, three standing stones, 2.7, 1.3 and 2 metres apart and 13.65 metres from a low stone set on edge—77.5cms/24.7cms.

141. LAURAGH LOWER: Fort—83cms/22.5cms.

142. SHRONEBIRRA: "Stone circle"—circle of standing stones from which some of the stones appear to have been removed—64.8cms/.5cms.

143. GORTAVALLIG: "Killeenagh Burial Ground (Children's Disused)" 76.5cms/2cms.

144. KILMAKILLOGE:	"Kilmakilloge Church (in ruins) Grave Yd." This graveyard contains the tomb of the McFinian Dhu, last chief of the Kerry branch of the O'Sullivans Beare—58.5cms/47.5cms.
145. DERRYRUSH:	"Loughmackeenlaun. Well (site of)" Rounds were made here up to within living memory and it was said there were islands which moved around the lake. The lake is now much reduced in size by drainage. When the writer enquired locally for the well he was told "the lake was the well," but he found in the position where the site of the well is marked on the map a circular mound, 2/3 metres in height, on which there are a number of stones, both loose and built into the mound, which is too overgrown to determine if these stones were the remains of a building or not. However, on one of the stones was cut a rude cross, similar to others in places where "rounds" were made—Lake 61.5cms/49cms. Site of well 62cms/48.5cms.
146. COLLORUS :	"Burial Ground (Site of)" Not seen by the writer.—36cms/27.5cms.

Map No. 111

| 147. GLANMORE: | "Gallauns"—large standing stone, now fallen, 2.6 metres away from which are three standing stones standing at right angles to each other, with a boulder, possibly the capstone, within. The stones seem to the writer too large for a wedge grave and look to him more like a portal dolmen. 71.5cms/34cms. |

The writer feels he should mention the finely sited stone circles at Drombohilly (Grid Reference V790 609) and Dromoghty, Dowros, (Grid Reference V880 655), but here he is getting into country with which he is not well acquainted so, feeling rather as Charles Kingsley felt about his

Westward Ho "only half as good as I could have written and only one hundredth part as good as ought to be written on the matter," he closes his list.

While obviously any survey of this area should include Bere Island the writer has to confess, with regret, that he has not yet succeeded in doing any exploration of this island. On the map (Sheet No. 128) he finds:

"Killeenagh Fort" at CLOONAGHLIN WEST (38cms/49cms)

"Gallaun" at Coomastooka, in Greenane townland (57.5cms/55cms) and

"Gallaun" in Ballynakilla townland (42.5cms/56cms).

Captain T.M. Keogh, in his pamphlet "A Short Account of the History and Antiquities of Bere Island and Berehaven" says of the first that "it is a genuine rath but that very little of it remains," and it is probably the fort mentioned by Westropp (JRSAI No. 50) as "Killeenagh Gobbeen." Both Westropp and Captain Keogh mention the "gallaun" at Coomastooka, while of that at Ballynakilla Captain Keogh says (1913) "there is one of these stones and the remaining stump of a second; but within the memory of man there were three" and Westropp (1919) says that there is one standing stone and two stumps here. Westropp also writes of "two stumps near the road eastward of the school and a fallen one, $8\frac{1}{2}$ feet long, on the hill above Shee Head," but these are not mentioned by Keogh nor are they marked on the map. Keogh says there is a small circle on the isthmus joining the promontory of Doonbeg (43cms/38cms) and refers to that promontory as "evidently at one time the great natural stronghold of Bere Island" whereas Westropp does not mention this circle of standing stones but does refer to Doonbeg as a promontory fort and he also mentions the promontory fort of Doonigar (9cms/45cms).

The most important site on Bere Island would seem to be that to which Captain Keogh refers as a "quite abnormal specimen of cromlech, close to a lane running from the naval rifle range to Rerrin village." The writer has been told that this is a very fine example of a wedge grave, but, again, this is not marked on the map.

To come to more modern times, it may be of interest to record that Captain Keogh says there were four martello towers on Bere Island, two of which are still standing, one at Ardagh, north of the old road above Ballynakilla (69cms/59cms) and one at Cloonaghlin. The other two were one at Rerrin, demolished to build the redoubt there and one at Ardaragh removed to make room for Lonehort Battery. He also mentions that the signal tower, now in ruins, which is in sight of similar ones on Sheeps Head, Dursey Island and Blackball Head, was built at the same time as the martello towers.

While he was sent on many a "wild goose chase" the writer is grateful to the many local people who have assisted him in his search and he was particularly impressed by the interest shown by young people and would like to express his thanks to Masters Michael Collins, Kevin O'Shiel, Finbar McCarthy, John Joe O'Sullivan and Miss Noreen O'Sullivan for the help they have given him in the field; but for their sharp sight many a monument would have been missed.

The writer observes that he has omitted one site on Map No. 102 "LACKERAGH—" "Burial Gd" (85cms/54cms), in which there is a tombstone inscribed "In memory of John Broderick sail maker of Gosport in the county of Hants, England, who died at sea on board R.Y.S. Helen and was buried here August 21 1869."

ADDENDUM

Since the foregoing list was prepared by the writer the following sites have been brought to his notice.

Map No. 114

148. KNOCKOURA: Very doubtful site; three small standing stones in a row, 1m and 75m apart, with a small slab standing on edge at an angle of forty five degrees to and 2.5m from these. 74cms/4cms.

149. DOONEEN: Two low ring forts in poor condition, close by each other. In one there are signs of a souterrain and the other one is very much overgrown. They are close to the Allihies/ Eyeries road but hidden from it by a copper mines reservoir. Perhaps they may be the Dooneen mentioned by Westropp (JRSAI Vol. 51) but the writer feels they could not qualify for the term "promontory fort." 24cms/15cms.

150. KILCATHERINE: Small standing stone 1m by 1.2m beside which is a recumbent stone (possibly fallen) 2.70m by .60.m. 68cms/30cms. About two hundred metres from the above is another small standing stone 1.3m by 1.15m. 66.5cms/31cms. These stand on a high ridge overlooking site No. 118, **Kilcatherine Wedge Grave.**

Map No. 126

151. GARNISH: **Excellent example of a boulder dolmen,** near to Site No. 114 Ballynacarriga, to which site, hitherto regarded as doubtful, it would seem to give authenticity. 65.5cms/34cms. The writer is grateful to Mr. Sean O'Nuallain for bringing this site to his attention.

APPENDIX B

THE WORKS OF STANDISH O'GRADY

Scintilla Shelleiana, ed. Arthur Clive, Dublin, 1875.
History of Ireland: the Heroic Period, vol. I, Dublin, 1878.
Early Bardic Literature, Dublin, 1879.
History of Ireland: Cuculain and His Contemporaries, vol. II, Dublin, 1880.
History of Ireland; Critical and Philosophical, vol. I, Dublin, 1881.
The Crisis in Ireland, Dublin, 1882.
Cuculain: an Epic, Dublin, 1882.
Toryism and the Tory Democracy, London, 1886.
Red Hugh's Captivity, London, 1889.
Finn and His Companions, London, 1892.
The Bog of Stars, London, 1893.
The Story of Ireland, London, 1894.
The Coming of Cuculain, London, 1894.
Lost on Du Corrig, London, 1894.
The Chain of Gold, London, 1895.
In the Wake of King James, London, 1896.
Pacata Hibernia, ed., London, 1896.
Ulrick the Ready, London, 1896.
The Flight of the Eagle, London, 1897.
All Ireland, Dublin, 1898.
The Queen of the World, London, 1900.
In the Gates of the North, Kilkenny, 1901.
Ideals in Ireland (in collaboration), London, 1901.
Hugh Roe O'Donnell: a Sixteenth Century Irish Historical Play, Belfast, 1902.
The Mask of Finn, Kilkenny, 1907.
The Departure of Dermot, Dublin, 1917.
The Passing of Cuculain, Dublin, 1917.

NOTES

Abbreviations

JCHAS   Journal of the Cork Historical and Archaeological Society
JKAHS   Journal of the Kerry Archaeological and Historical Society
JRSAI   Journal of the Royal Society of Antiquaries of Ireland
PRIA   Proceedings of the Royal Irish Academy

Introduction

1   James Hogan, 'The Tricha cet and Related Land Measures', *PRIA* vol. 38 section C (August 1929).
2   Charles Smith, *The Ancient and Present State of the County and City of Cork*, 2 vols. 1750 (Cork, 1893 ed.) vol. 1, p. 272.
3   A. Farrington, 'The Glaciation of the Bantry Bay District', *Scientific Proceedings, Royal Dublin Society* (1936); K. Coe and E.B. Selwood, 'The Upper Palaeozoic Stratigraphy of West Cork and Parts of South Kerry', *PRIA* vol. 66 section B (May 1968).

Chapter 1

1   William Makepeace Thackeray, *The Irish Sketch Book* (London: Smith, Elder & Co., 1877), p. 348.
2   Mr. & Mrs. S.C. Hall, *Ireland: Its Scenery, Character etc.* (London, 1841), vol. 1, p.154.
3   Horatio Townsend, *A General and Statistical Survey of the County of Cork* (Dublin, 1810), p. 393.
4   T.M. Keogh, *A Short Account of the History and Antiquities of Bere Island and Berehaven* (Bournemouth: Pardy & Son, 1913), p. 30.
5   Sean O'Coindealbhain, 'The United Irishmen in County Cork', *JCHAS* vol. 53 No. 178 (1948), p. 123.
6   Ibid, p. 119.
7   De Latocnaye, *A Frenchman's Walk through Ireland, 1796-97*, trans. John Stevenson (Dublin & London, 1917), p. 92.
8   P. Brendan Bradley, *Bantry Bay* (London: Williams & Northgate, 1931), p. 241.

Chapter 2

1   John T. Collins, 'The O'Crowleys of Coill t-Sealbhaigh', *JCHAS* vol. 57 no. 185 (1953), p. 33.

2-4 Robert Dunlop, *Ireland under the Commonwealth*, 2 vols. (Manchester University Press, 1913), vol. 2, pp. 457, 425, 327.

5 Charles McNeill, 'Reports on the Rawlinson Collection of Manuscripts Preserved in the Bodleian Library, Oxford', *Analecta Hibernica* no. 1 (March 1930), p. 28.

6 Bishop Dive Downes, 'Visitation of His Diocese, 1699-1702', ed. T.A. Lunham, *JCHAS* vol. 15 (1909), p. 164.

Chapter 3

1 D. Maddison O'Brien, 'Two Crosses at Crooha West, Adrigole', *JCHAS* vol. 73 (1968), p. 71.

2 *Proceedings of the Royal Society of Antiquaries of Scotland* vol. 10 4th series (1912), p. 279.

3 Smith, *Cork*, vol. 1, p. 18.

4 Ibid, p. 274.

5 Pádraig O Maidín, 'Pococke's Tour of Ireland and South-West Ireland in 1758', *JCHAS* vol. 63 no. 198 (1958), pp. 89-90.

6 De Latocnaye, *Frenchman's Walk*, p. 96.

7 Townsend, *Cork*, pp. 395, 394.

8 Owen Connellan, trans., *The Annals of Ireland* (Dublin, 1846), p. 1581; J. O'Donovan, ed., *Annals of Ireland by the Four Masters*, 7 vols. (Dublin, 1856), vol. 7, p. 1763; Philip O'Sullivan Beare, *Historiae Catholicae Iberniae* (Lisbon, 1621), trans. Matthew J. Byrne as *A History of Ireland under Elizabeth* (Dublin: Sealy, Bryers & Walker, 1903).

Chapter 4

1 The account of Fontaine's life in Ch. 4 is based on James Fontaine, *Memoirs of a Huguenot Family*, trans. Ann Maury (New York: Putnam, 1853).

2 Dive Downes, 'Visitation', p. 164.

3 Sir Arthur Vicars, *Index to the Prerogative Wills of Ireland, 1536-1810* (Dublin: Ponsonby, 1897).

Chapter 5

1 Bede, *History of the English Church and People*, trans. Leo Sherley-Price (Harmondsworth: Penguin, 1955), p. 53.

2 O Dubhagain, Seaán Mór and O'Huidhrin, Giolla-na-Naomh *Topographical Poems*, ed. James Carney (Dublin Institute for Advanced Studies, 1943).

3   Jeremiah J. O'Mahony, *West Cork and Its Story*, 1961 (Cork, 1975 ed.), p. 37.
4-5 Ibid, pp. 38, 39.
6   D.A. Binchy, 'Patrick and His Biographers, Ancient and Modern', *Studia Hibernica* 2 (1962).
7   J. Coombes, 'The Benedictine Priory of Ross', *JCHAS* vol. 73 no. 218 (1968), p. 155.
8   Aubrey Gwynn and R.N. Hadcock, *Medieval Religious Houses: Ireland* (London, 1970), p. 391.
9   John Lyons, 'Local Names', *JCHAS* vol. 3 no. 25 (1894), p. 112.

Chapter 6

1   J.P. Prendergast, *Letter to the Earl of Bantry, or, a warning to English purchasers of the perils of the Irish Incumbered Estate Court, exemplified in the purchase by Lord Charles Pelham Clinton M.P. of two estates in the Barony of Bere, County of Cork* (Dublin, 1854).
2   Alfred Webb, *Compendium of Irish Biography* (Dublin, 1878), p. 9; see also Lodge's *Peerage of Ireland* on Barnwall Viscounts Kingslands.
3   Matthew O'Reilly, 'The Barnwalls', *Records of the Meath Archaeological Society (Riocht na Mide)* vol. 1 no. 3 (1957), p. 64.
4   S.B. Barnwall, *Irish Genealogist* vol. 3 no. 4 (July 1959), p. 124.

Chapter 7

1   James Morrin, *Calendar of the Patent and Close Rolls of Chancery in Ireland in the Reign of Elizabeth* (1861 ed.), 1594 no. 2, p. 266.
2   Carew Mss 1611.
3   Dive Downes, 'Visitation', p. 165.
4   Sile Ni' Chinneide, 'A New View of 18th-Century Life in Kerry', *JKAHS* no. 6 (1973), p. 84.
5   Ibid, p. 87.

Chapter 8

1   Lady Georgina Chatterton, *Rambles in the South of Ireland during the Year 1838*, 2 vols. (London: Saunders & Otley, 1839), vol. 1, p. 75.

Chapter 10

1   A.J. Fetherstonehaugh, 'The True Story of the Two Chiefs of Dunboy', *JRSAI* vol. 4 (1894), p. 35.

2 Ibid, pp. 139-140.
3 PRO 20 March 1912.
4 PRO 7 December 1830.

Chapter 11

1 Thomas Johnson Westropp, 'The Promontory Forts of Beare and Bantry, Part 2', *JRSAI* vol. 50 (1921), p. 10.
2 Keogh, Bere Island, p. 34.
3 Wych Mss 170 PROI.

Chapter 12

1 Richard N. Hoskyn, *Sailing Directions for the Coast of Ireland* (London, 1887), p. 28.
2 John O'Donoghue, *In a Quiet Land* (London: Batsford, 1957), p. 191.
3 Cathaldus Giblin, 'Catalogue of Material of Irish Interest in the Collection Nunziatura di Fiandra Vatican Archives', *Collectanea Hibernica* no. 4 (1961).
4 Chatterton, *Rambles*, vol. 1, pp. 75-76.
5-6 Robert Kane, *The Industrial Resources of Ireland* (Dublin: Hodge & Smith, 1845), pp. 195-196.

Chapter 13

1 Rupert Jones. List of Royal Naval Ships quoted in letter dated 22 March 1976, National Maritime Museum, Greenwich, London.
2 Felix Riesenberg, *Cape Horn* (London: Robert Hale, 1941), p. 217.
3 Louis M. Cullen, 'Privateers Fitted Out in Irish Ports in the 18th Century', *Irish Sword* vol. 3 no. 12 (1958), p. 176.
4 Dive Downes, 'Visitation', p. 167.

Chapter 14

1 Maire MacNeill, *The Festival of Lughnasa. A Study of the Survival of the Celtic Festival of the Beginning of the Harvest* (Oxford University Press, 1962), pp. 160-161, 186, 406, 573, 412-413.
2 Lyons, 'Local Names', p. 112.
3 *Calendar of Papal Letters* vol. 8, p. 424.
4 Carew Mss 107 Henry VIII.
5 Westropp, 'Promontory Forts', vol. 51 (1921), p. 4.
6 O Maidín, 'Pococke's Tour', p. 87.

7   Ibid, p. 81.
8   Townsend, *Cork*, p. 395.
9   Smith, *Cork*, p. 12.
10 'Fishing Rights off Coast of Ireland 1625', Calendar Carew Mss State Papers Ireland 1647-60, pp. 56-57.
11 *Calendar of State Papers Elizabeth 1592*, pp. 11-12.
12 A.J. Went, 'Pilchards in the South of Ireland', *JCHAS* vol. 1 (1946), pp. 137-157.
13 Hoskyn, *Sailing Directions*, p. 33.
14 Henry William Edmund Lansdowne, *Glanerought and the Petty Fitzmaurices by the Marquess of Lansdowne* (Oxford, 1937).
15 Fr. O'Sullivan, 'Ancient History of Kerry', *JCHAS* vol. 6 (1900), p. 16.

BIBLIOGRAPHY

Barrington, T.J., *Discovering Kerry*, Dublin: Blackwater Press, 1976.

Barry, John G., 'The Norman Invasion of Ireland', *JCHAS* vol. 75 no. 222 (1970), pp. 105-124.

Bowen, E.G., *Saints, Seaways and Settlements*, Cardiff: University of Wales Press, 1977.

Brady, W. Maziere, *Clerical and Parochial Records of Cork, Cloyne and Ross*, 3 vols., Dublin, 1863.

Brenan, M.J., *An Ecclesiastical History of Ireland*, Dublin: James Duffy, 1840.

Brewer's Dictionary of Phrase and Fable.

Burke's Landed Gentry of Great Britain and Ireland, 1886, 1958, 1970 eds.

Butler, William F.T., *Gleanings from Irish History*, London, 1925.

Carew, P.J., *Ecclesiastical History of Ireland*, Dublin, 1835.

Carney, James, *The Problem of St. Patrick*, Dublin Institute for Advanced Studies, 1961.

Dictionary of National Biography.

Du Maurier, Daphne, *Hungry Hill*, London: Victor Gollancz, 1943.

Ferguson, Lady Mary Catherine, *The Story of the Irish before the Conquest*, Dublin, 1867; 3rd ed. Dublin: Sealy, Bryers & Walker, 1903.

Fetherstonehaugh, A.J., 'The True Story of the Two Chiefs of Dunboy', *JRSAI* vol. 4 (1894), pp. 34-43, 139-149.

Firth, Charles H., *Cromwell's Army* London: Methuen, 1902.

Fitzgerald, Walter, *The Historical Geography of Early Ireland*, London: George Philip & Son, 1925.

Froude, J.A., *The Two Chiefs of Dunboy*, London: Longman's, Green & Co., 1889.

Harden, Donald, *The Phoenicians*, London: Thames & Hudson, 1962.

Haverty, Martin, *The History of Ireland, Ancient and Modern*, Dublin, 1860.

Hutchins' Family Papers, Ardnagashel.

Ireland, John de Courcy, 'Robert Halpin and the Great Eastern', *Technology Ireland* (November 1973).

Jones, E.H. Stuart, *An Invasion That Failed: the French Expedition to Ireland, 1796*, Oxford, 1950.

Kenney, James F., *The Sources for the Early History of Ireland: Ecclesiastical*, New York: Columbia University Press, 1929.

Lewis, Samuel, *A Topographical Dictionary of Ireland*, London, 1837.

Mac Cárthaigh, Mícheál, 'Placenames of the Parish of Kilnamanagh', *Dinnseanchas* vol. 6 nos. 1-2 (1974).

Lodge, John, *Peerage of Ireland*, 7 vols., Dublin, 1789.

McGee, Thomas D'Arcy, *A Popular History of Ireland: From the Earliest Period to the Emancipation of the Catholics*, 2 vols., New York, 1865.

MacLaren, Moray, *Bonnie Prince Charlie*, London: Hart-Davis, 1972.

MacLean, Sir John, ed., *The Life and Times of Sir Peter Carew*, London, 1857.

MacLysaght, Edward, *The Surnames of Ireland*, Dublin: Irish Academic Press, 1973.

MacNeill, Eoin, *Saint Patrick*, Dublin, 1934.

Neeson, Eoin, *The First Book of Irish Myths and Legends*, Cork: Mercier Press, 1965.

O'Brien, Conor, *The Runaways*, London: Harrap, 1941.

O'Connor Morris, William, *Ireland 1494 to 1868*, Cambridge University Press, 1909.

O'Grady, Hugh Art, *Standish James O'Grady. The Man and The Writer*, Dublin & Cork: Talbot Press, 1929.

O'Halloran, W. *Early Irish History and Antiquities and the History of West Cork*, Dublin, 1916.

O'Mahony, John, 'Morty Oge O'Sullivan, Captain of the Wild Geese', *JCHAS* vol. 1A (1892), pp. 95-99.

Orpen, G.H., *Ireland under the Normans, 1169-1333*, 4 vols., Oxford: Clarendon Press, 1911-20.

Pettigrew & Oulton, *Dublin Almanac & General Register*, 1845.

Prendergast, J.P., *The Cromwellian Settlement in Ireland*, London, 1870.

Smiles, Samuel, *The Huguenots in England and Ireland*, London: John Murray, 1889.

Somerville, Boyle T., 'Prehistorics', *JCHAS* vol. 33 (1928), pp. 57-68.

Somerville, Boyle T., 'The Spanish Expedition to Ireland 1601', *Irish Sword* vol. 7 no. 26 (Summer 1965).

Sullivan, T.D., *Bantry, Berehaven and the O'Sullivan Sept*, Dublin: Sealy, Bryers & Walker, 1908.

Thomas, Albert, *Wait and See*, London: Michael Joseph, 1944.

Thom's Irish Almanac and Official Directory for the Year 1910, Dublin, 1910.

Webster, Charles A., 'The Diocese of Ross', *JCHAS* vol. 29 (1924), pp. 35-37.

Webster, Charles A., *The Diocese of Ross, Its Bishops, Clergy and Parishes*, Cork ,1936.

Williams, Jeremy, 'Dunboy Castle', *Architectural Review* no. 930 (August 1974).

Names Index